Ann's Letters

Ann's Letters

A Newly Released Collection of Letters
from the American Civil War

Gerald Dougherty

iUniverse LLC
Bloomington

ANN'S LETTERS
A Newly Released Collection of Letters from the American Civil War

iUniverse books may be ordered through booksellers or by contacting:

iUniverse LLC
1663 Liberty Drive
Bloomington, IN 47403
www.iuniverse.com
1-800-Authors (1-800-288-4677)

ISBN: 978-1-4917-1619-9 (sc)
ISBN: 978-1-4917-1620-5 (e)

Library of Congress Control Number: 2013921371

Printed in the United States of America.

iUniverse rev. date: 02/07/2014

Table of Contents

About The Author

GERALD DOUGHERTY

Jerry

is a Northern-bred, Technical Engineer, Analytical, and a Southern Transplant for 40 years, Patriotic, with an Understanding of-, and Respect for-, Family Dedication and Sacrifices in the Commitment to Support their Troops and Ideals. He is retired in Atlanta, GA, with his wife of 56 years, where they enjoy their four married children and six grand-children.

Although he was born, trained, and started his life and family in the North, he has also loved living in the South. This has helped him learn the cultures of both the North and the South to relate to the Civil War.

This collection shows us some of the "Real" thoughts and actions basic to everyone, in Family Life. It also punctuates the importance of Family and Friends, and the support they provide, in stressful times.

Jerry

knows that today's families are NOT much different from those of 150 years ago.

Thank You

I am pleased, while writing this volume, to have the belated opportunity to thank Eve Ann Huffman, who was a young woman during the Civil War, for saving this collection of Civil War Letters.

Did she have an uncanny foresight for saving historical items, or, as was really more likely, was she merely a young girl with a passion for saving all of the letters she received? (Letter writing was a rapidly-developing skill at this time, and mail services were meager, at best. It is amazing that letters to and from soldiers got delivered at all.)

Or, perhaps, did she save some of the letters because they included the words of guidance from, and connections to, her two older brothers?

We will never know her reasons, for certain, but we all greatly appreciate her care in saving the mementoes from her corner of history.

Thanks, too, to her daughter-in-law, Becky Dougherty Bowman, who carried the later responsibility of passing them along to our Mother, Lillian Thomas Dougherty, who then saw them safely to us.

The letters have suffered no significant casualty in the 150 years of their existence because of the careful handling by each of these folks. Despite an 80-year period when the letters were stored in the upstairs of a weather-exposed barn in central Ohio, and couldn't enjoy air-conditioning until the late 1980's, they have survived in surprisingly good condition.

I thank, too, the contribution of a distant cousin, Jim Dohren, in separately copying and transcribing many of the letters for our separate purposes.

Special thanks to my granddaughter, Gentry Susan Moore, for her guidance in designing the cover for the book.

I give my sincere thanks and gratitude to Mr. Gordon Jones and Ms. Sue Ver Hoev of the Atlanta History Center for their encouragement to publish these letters for past, present and future students of the Civil War.

Thanks are in order, as well, to the many others who have expressed their support and sentiments during the preparation of this volume. I have appreciated your enthusiasm.

THANK YOU!

—

Introduction

"ANN'S LETTERS" began as a collection of hand-written letters from Civil War Troops, their families and friends. While "translating" the originals I realized that they represented a wide variety of levels of education, and verbal skills, during an era when formal schooling was still limited.

I have presented the translation in the same visual layout as the originals, so that the reader may easily compare them with the pictures of the originals.

The letters serve as chapters of this book, since no other separation seems logical.

I have deliberately included my "sic" notes to allow the reader to fully experience the feeling of the letters, as well as the translation, and to assist the reader in his understanding. Spelling corrections, too, have been included to improve the reading speed. Notes and expansions of subject matter within the letters are included with the appropriate letters throughout the text. While removing such matter to a remote section is possible, it serves my purpose to have it more easily available to the reader to enhance his reading comprehension.

Most of the letters are written (as they were taught in that era) with several oft-repeated phrases at the beginnings, which proved to be "cookie-cutter" formalities, regarded as "proper" etiquette in letter writing. Some of these depended upon the area, "school", and teacher from whom they learned. Most of these statements have been later abandoned as superfluous fluff. These take the form of, . . .

"Dear Sir, it is with pleasure that I seat my sealf (sic) (self) this rainy morning to let you now (sic) (know) that I am well and I hope when these few lines come to hand they will find you in the same greate (sic) (great) blefsing (sic) (blessing) of health", . . . or . . . , "I seat mysealf(sic) (self) this monday morning to take my pen in hand to send you a few lines to tell you that I am well at preasent (sic) (present) and have mostly gotten over my fever that had me disabled for nearly 3 (sic) (three) weeks but that I am able to get out again and will return to my reg't as soon as next week. I hope these few lines find you in the same blefsing (sic) (blessing) of good health and well-being"

By the time a soldier in the field used this format ten times in his letter-writing, he could have run short of paper, or run out of ink!! We have become used to, "Dear Jeff, . . ," and, "Sincerely, . . .", or, "Miss you."

As the reader discovers, if he were not aware of the writings of an earlier era, many improvements have been put into practice, including the replacing of ". . . fs" with "ss", in words such as "mess, cross, and blessing". Young readers may not be aware of these basic era-based differences from our modern language. I felt that including these in my book made sense, since it is considering letters written in the 1860's, 150 years ago, from the perspective of people of 150 years ago.

Having been a teacher of speed reading, I have tried to make the text as easily understood as I could and shown the corrected words in parentheses so the reader can proceed without having to stop to determine the intended word, which I have already done for him.

Since I am not a practicing Historian, I have:

translated the letters for their content.
related to their historical references in a few cases, from broad and readily available sources.

tied the letters in to the events and locations of the War as needed.

expanded background information to provide the reader a better feeling of the situations of the writers

let the letters convey the urgencies and concerns of the writers as they experienced the realities around them.

In general, I allowed the letters to create the scenes described by the writers, and hope you feel I have succeeded.

As you proceed, you will see that life was hard at home as well as at the front. If you were a woman at home with seven small children, a farm to run, and elders to look after, how would you react when they all got sick with typhoid fever, or diphtheria, and your man was away at war? Many survived just such situations, but with sickness and death all around!

ANN'S LETTERS present many views and insights of life at home as well as first hand reports from the Front.

The background of family and neighborhood events included here brings to life the complex stresses being endured by the troops as they waged war for their Nation at a relatively great distance from home.

The writers describe a number of devastating diseases, frequently births, and deaths, family concerns, and worry about their crops. They provide willing support to each other by words and prayers. Neighbors help each other as best they can.

Letters from the troops give some light on the war, but also highlight their worry and need-for-news about their loved ones back home.

The troops try to maintain their family duties of advising wives and guiding children while still concentrating on their own duties of war. Their concerns,—humble,—heart-felt, and—patriotic—, are voiced freely. Support of others in the letters is asked-for-, and received.

Spiritual guidance is freely given, where it is needed, as if the troops were still at home.

The study of ANN'S LETTERS has led in a number of interesting directions as new information was digested.

One of the featured troops was killed **after** the end of the War, and never made it back home!

A famous depiction of one of the prisoners-of-war is **debunked** by new direct evidence revealed here.

Letters presented here that are relevent to other specific persons and groups are being sent directly to those resources for their archives.

I have tried to weave a fabric around the troops and their families to complete an humble tapestry of their times.

The fabric of their family lives and interactions is not a great deal different from ours, disregarding the technology differences between the times. Without autos, phones, TV, radios, computers, baseball, movies and electricity, their needs and ours are quite similar. Simpler times, but the importance of freedom and patriotism was somewhat more pronounced, as was their obvious desire to vote.

These letters paint an indelible picture of the affects that families had on their troops and the importance that caring words, prayers and support provided to them.

A final strong feeling of relief is expressed by one of the ladies at home; ". . . **GLORY to GOD the WAR is OVER!**"

As you continue to read through these letters, recognize that they are Preserved, Personal, Private, Previously un-Published, at the same time, Priviledged and Public. (The fact of priviledge refers to their closeness to Gen. Sherman's Headquarters Company, where troops have, first-hand, heard and experienced the things they relate.) Hopefully, you will find these letters useful to your studies of the Civil War and learn more of the families who were supporting them from Home.

I Invite You To:

Peer through the unique windows of Life at Home for troops fighting the Civil War

Discover what the families faced while Dads and Brothers were away

Experience the threats of diseases on every side with births and deaths, and misery, a part of every day

Imagine the anxiety hoping your loved ones are OK

Appreciate the support of friends and neighbors, which was needed to survive

Congratulate the heroes, often being the wives and children, who kept the homes and the community safe

Thank the troops who fought to defend their beliefs

Bless the Patriots who helped the U.S. evolve and become stronger

Honor those who saved the letters we used to understand both the troops and families, so we could . . .

Look through these windows of **OUR HISTORY**

Relive their lives as the letters come alive

Compare your life today with the families of the 1860's

The Letters

This collection of Eve Ann Huffman's American Civil War letters came from Northern Troops, in the service, and their families and friends in Ohio and Indiana, during 1862 through 1865. It encompasses their involvements in the 126th Ohio Volunteer Infantry (OVI), the 51st Ohio Veteran Volunteer Infantry (OVVI), as it became known, and the 85th Indiana Volunteer Infantry, during the Civil War.

Eve Ann (Ann) was a 21-year old girl, living in a small farming town in Central Ohio, whose letters from her two brothers and two friends came straight from the War.

She, being quite well-educated, with her generation's passion to write and communicate by letter, relayed these about the community, and stayed in touch with many area friends, as well, giving us a broad view of the lives of the families at home.

Her brothers had been school teachers, with the skills to describe the scenes and the events around them.

Two of the troops were friends of Ann, who seemed, also, somewhat smitten with her. References to other local men who were serving at the same time, broaden the contacts throughout the community.

While the soldiers were fighting the War, the wives and families endured sickness and stress, fighting to hold their lives together on their farms and at home. The stresses of war and homefront were endured through mutual letters of advice, compassion, friendship and love. If life was hard at the "Front", it was often unimaginable at home!

NOTE:

This collection has survived because Eve Ann (Ann) saved whatever letters she got, and later passed them along to her daughter-in-law, Rebecca Dougherty Bowman. They then went to her grand niece-in-law, Lillian Thomas Dougherty, and were passed on to her son, Gerald Dougherty, the author.

I hope you will agree that what you find here, only now being released, will prove desirable for study by students and Patrons of the Civil War on the occasion of its Sesqui-Centennial Anniversary.

This is the only known photo of Eve Ann Huffman and was determined to have been taken when she was in her early fifties, in the early 1890's, after her children were grown. As was the custom, she is wearing a clothing style typical of her age and she appears older than she would have appeared today.

IN THIS COLLECTION we follow the experiences of several soldiers who are merely writing to the folks back home to keep in touch during the Civil War.

Two of them are brothers, John J., and David L. Huffman, both of the 85th Indiana Volunteer Infantry, who have family and friends in both Ohio and Indiana. They travel together throughout most of the war and are not separated until late in the War.

Another, William Bowman, lives in New Cumberland, Ohio, (Tuscarawas County), where parts of the Huffman family also reside, and who, though unrelated to each other, have close ties. He is enlisted in the 126th Ohio Volunteer Infantry, a regiment formed in Tuscarawas County, and into which a number of his area friends have also joined.

The fourth is Joseph W. Kimmel, a casual friend from neighboring Carroll County, who writes to family and friends to keep in touch, and who is enlisted in the 51st Ohio Volunteer Infantry.

Most of the letters in the collection have been saved by a sister of the Huffmans, Eve Anne, who actively writes to the servicemen, and passes their thoughts, wishes, and feelings along to others in the families and the community. She is a prolific writer, who communicates and speaks well for the period.

A second sister, Christine (Chrissey) Huffman, is unmarried, and also sends letters to the many servicemen from the area, and to their families.

The Huffmans entered the war in August, 1862, enlisting in Fort Wayne, Indiana, and Ashboro, Indiana, although part of their family lives in Ohio.

William Bowman entered on August 4th, 1862, and immediately found himself in Parkersburgh, Wood County,

Virginia, (now West Virginia) under the command of Captain Oliver Franc(e).

Joseph W. Kimmel, although also from the same general area as the others, (Carroll County, Ohio, adjacent to Tuscarawas County), becomes assigned to the 51st OVI and his fortunes take him to different campaigns during the war.

Eve Anne Huffman, hereafter known as "Ann", also saved a few letters from her youngest brother, Daniel. He was, as well, a very available young man who was known by several of the girls in the area, probably from church, or school, as the community appears to have been rather close. Those who lived here had extended portions of their families "nearby", when nearby might have been several miles distant, or further.

One of the local girls at home had sent a casual letter (on Dec 16th 1861) to Ann's brother, Daniel, stating that she is now a teacher ((which he already knows)), in a pleasant school, and that she has thirty six students and expects to "get a few more in a few days." She goes on to say, "I have not been so badly beaten since that night & hope you have not but it was alright in the morning. That's so. I would like very much to see you I was at home on Friday night and came back on Saturday evening. The folks here are talking about going down to the camp ((sugaring camp, where the community collects tree sap and makes sugar)) when there comes a good snow. George Dakuff is going to take us all down in the sled. If you hear of it come and go with us. I do not know whether it will be asking too much or not if I ask you for your likeness ((picture)). If so, I hope you will pardon me. I would like you would come up and see my school It is real nice There is two such pretty girls here & boys too. I have not time to write much more at present as I am going to send it to the office just now Write soon & direct to New Harrisburgh, Carroll County Ohio.

Maggie J. Harper ((to)) Daniel Huffman"

NOTES: (Letter A)

This gives us an idyllic look at what their world was like before the war, and indicates the mobility of the young folks starting their careers and having to move from their family homes to a distance for their job. Many folks of this era stayed on the family farm, or didn't migrate far from home. We don't really know what would have been worthy of causing her to be beaten, and we can only surmise what actions were involved, but it apparently involved him, since she refers to "that night". It is right after this time that they get fully involved in the stirrings of the war and the demands of the approaching wartime.

A-1

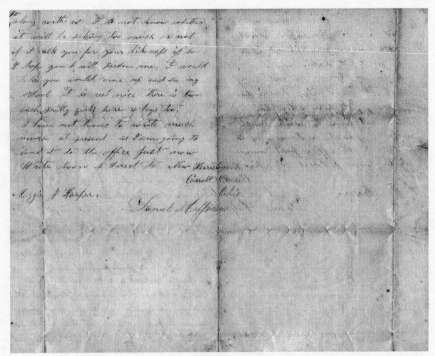

A-2

Letter 1

The first soldier letter is a note in Sept 1862 from William Bowman to his friend David Huffman, uncle of the two Huffman boys, who later enlisted ((as above)) in the 85th Indiana Volunteer Infantry.

William describes the conditions within the camp, so far, and how they got there. He claims, "I think by the grace of God I will get home safe but if I do not get home to see you I hope to meat (sic) you in heaven There is a good deal of bad conduct here but Wes ((friend Hoopingarner)) and I do not take any part in it and I thank god (sic) for it that he will protect us from any harm I think he will help us from being hurt we have to be very strict here what we drink for there was a man poisand (sic) here last night on whiskey but Wesley and I do not drink of the filthy stuff (sic) for tell the folks that I like it verry (sic) well here tell the boys . . . that I would like to see them tell them that I will come home next spring the war will be at home tell our girls to be contented for I will see them again and and (sic,) ((written twice)) live with them I must bring my letter to a close this lett(sic) is not wrote (sic) very plain let some of the boys read it if you can not write as soon as you get this letter and tell me how you are getting along I heard that you was a coming to Camp Steubenville to see me but was to (sic) late for we went away that day that Davy was here I wish you had come with them to see us but you was to (sic) late we are about three hundred miles from home. we came about five hundred miles to get here the river is to (sic) low to come on it we rode it on the cars write as soon as you get this letter direct to Camp Parkersburgh Wood County Virginia in care of Captain Oliver Franc 126th Regiment (OVI)

William Bowman (to) David Huffman"

NOTES: (Letter 1)

Interesting comments on the characteristics of the people in camp,and almost raises some doubt as to whether he DOES protect himself from the evils of the camp, by his strong protestations! We later determined that he truly was as "heaven-motivated" as he professes, by his consistant later actions.

LTR1a

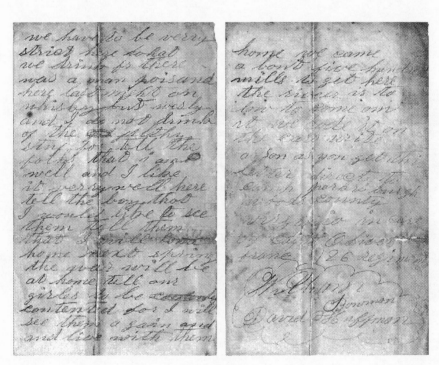

LTR1b

Letter 2

On September 24, 1862, William again wrote David Huffman, from Parkersburgh, to pass along some other information, including that "we expect an attack here soon . . . .".

Continuing, "for there was one hundred fifty cavalry men came in here to day and if they do come in on us they will haft (sic) to have a greate (sic) force we can have ten thousand of men here in five hours we have only two thousand here now, but there is two thousand on the other side of the river that is a laing (sic) in the ambush watching for them to cross the Canawway ((sic, probably the Little Kanawha)) and they will fire ((pg.2)) on them and we will come on them from this side We have ten peices (sic, pieces) of cannon came in here to day It will make a hard fight but I do not believe it at all for there is to (sic) big a force here The president procolamation (all sic) says that the war will be over in three months. If that is sow (sic) we will be at home soon The war can not last longer than spring. I think we will be in Parkersburgh all winter I have wrote you three or four letters and I have only got one (sic) I want you to write more to me for I want to now (sic) how you and the girls is a getting along and the nabours (sic) if they ar (sic) well ((pg.3)) I wrote John Mansfield one letter, and tell him to write to me as son (sic) as you get this letter and George Strawn to write to me for I would like to here(sic) from him and his family there is a greate (sic) deal of card playing a going on here but I have not touched a card since I have been in campe (sic) and I have not done any gambling here I dnot (sic) pay anny (sic) attention to them. I read my testament verry(sic) near evry (sic) night for (sic) I go to bed I try to do right I want you (sic) serve the lord with all your hart (sic) and I will try to do the same ((pg.4)) There is a great deal of wikedness (sic) in camp This a hard place to do right but I have to trust in the lord (sic) and he gives me grace I allways (sic) think he will save me from being kiled (sic) I must bring my letter to a close write to me soon as you get this letter Direct to Parkers burgh wood (sic) co Virginia in care of Capt Franc, 126th Regiment OVI

William Bowman
to Mr.David Huffman
W.B.D.H."

NOTES: (Letter 2)

The hand writing in this letter begins fairly neatly, but deteriorates gradually until it is quite messy as if the writer was running out of time, or getting more emotional as he wrote, although he states no reason in the letter. It also is quite orderly as if a lined under-page is used to guide the writer, until the last page where the straight lines degrade.

William assumes that the war can't last very long and that it should be over by spring. As many others, he also judged the intensity of the "uprising" as being less than it really was. The rebels' determination was underestimated as the War began.

LTR2a

there is a great deal of
wikedness in camp this
is a hard place to do
right but I have to put
my trust in the lord
and he gives me grace
I allways think he
will save me from
being killed I must
being my letter to a
close write as soon as you
get this letter direct
to parkers burgh wood
virginia
in care of capt
126 regiment france
William Bowman
to Mr David Hoffman
W B D H

September the
Mr David Hoffman Dear
Sir I take my pen in hand to
let you now that I am well
at present and I hope that these
few lines may find you in the
same blessing of health we are
par bersburgh in virginia
we expect an attack here
soon for there was one hundred
& fifty caualry men came in
here if they do
come on us they will haft
to have a great force we can
have ten thousand of men here
in five hours not only have
two thousand here now but
there is two thousand on the
other side of the river there is
a laying in the am both
watching for them to crass
the canaway and they will

file on them and we will
come on them from this
side ~~we have ten pieces~~
of cannon come in here
to day it will make a
hard fight but I do not
believe it at all for there
is to big a force here.
The president proclamation
says that the war will
be over in three months if
that is so we will be
at home soon the war can
not last longer then spring
I think we will stay in
parkers bush all winter
I have wrote you three or four
letters and I have only got on
I want you to write more
to me for I want to
now how you and the
girls is a getting along
and the nabours if they
ar well

I wrote John Mansfield one
letter and tell him if he got my
letter and tell him to write to
me as soon as you get this letter
and tell george strawn to write
to me and tell Mr.
strawn to write to me so
I would like to hear from
him and his family
there is a greate deal of
card playing a going on
here but I have not tuched
a card since I have ben in
campe and I have not done
any gambling here I dnot
pay anny attention to them
I read my testament
verry near every night
fore I goto bed I try
to do right I want you
serve the lord with all
your hart and I will
try to do the same

LTR2b

Letter 3

In the next four months, William's regiment moves over to Martinsburgh, Va., where he suggests his displeasure with having been forgotten by his friend, writing, on January the 28, AD 1863, "I have not received anny(sic) letter from you for a good while I would like to get word from you once more I tell you I am well satisfied in the army I have had my health verry (sic) well since I left home There is a good many sick in this regiment (pg.2) there is seven died out of our regiment there was two died out of our company last weeke (sic) we discharge (sic) Jhon (sic) Albaugh last night he has got palpitation of the heart I hope to god (sic) I will keep my health as well as I have I have mot (sic) much news to tell you Esra Albaugh is here to (sic) this morning He came after his son yesterday and he is a going to starte (sic) home withe (sic) to day

(pg.3) I do not want to get a discharge until the war is over if I keep my health I sent in my letter for you to send me some money in your next letter we have not anny money here we will get our money some time soon we will not get less than fifty or sixty dollars the next time and I will send you some I will make it all right when I get my money (pg.4) If you send me some money I want to xxxx(sic, crossout) have some money to get my boots half soled it takes one dollar for a pair of half soles I would like for you to send some in your next letter write as soon as tis (sic, this) comes to hand Direct to Martinsburgh Berkely Co (county) Virg (sic) Company G 126th reg OVI in care of Captain Gerome

William Bowman
David Huffman

Tell John Mansfield to write to me"

NOTE:(Letter 3)

Testy attitude due to no letters, showing how important news from home was to them. They are fighting without benefit of pay, for even the most important necessities. ((We are certain he is not blowing money on gambling, etc, because of the person he is)). He emphasizes the condition of the normal soldier in this war, perhaps a bit rag-tag at this time.

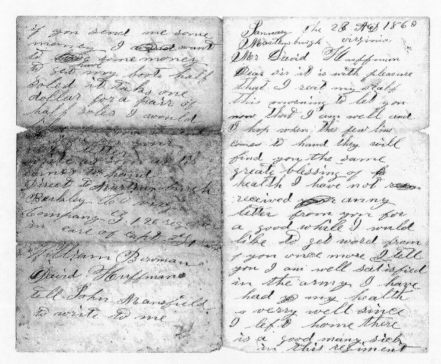

LTR3a

there is seven died
out of our regiment
There was two died
out of our company
last weeke we
discharge Thom Albaugh
last night he has
got the palpitation
of the heart
I hope to god I will
keep my health
as well as I have
I have not much
news to tell you
Esra Albaugh is
here to this morning
he came after
his son yesterday
and he is a going
to starte home
withe him to
day

I do not want
to get a discharge
till the war is over
if I keepe my
health & I sent
in my letter for
a you to send
me some money
in your next
letter we have
not anny money
here we will
get our money
some time soon
we will not get
less than
fifty or sixty
dollars the next
time and I will
send you some I
will make it all right
when I get my money

Letter 4

During this time, our first letter from John J. Huffman appears, addressed to his "Dear Brother", from a hospital in Danville, Ky., on February 13, 1863. ((It was located in a building that is, more recently, the Courthouse of Danville, Ky.))

On stationery emblazoned with a crowing rooster, and stating, "Cock-a-doodle-doo", attributed to J.R. Hawley, he shows a return address of "Hospital No. 1, 3rd Div of Ky Army, Danville, Ky, Feb 13 /63"

Going on, he states, "Dear Brother [he is writing here to the brother, Daniel, still at home, since his other brother David has been in the war with him,]

I neglected answering your letter of Dec 18th when I ought, and then I was taken down with a fever. therefore, I was unable to write. It was 4 weeks yesterday since I took sick. I had a pretty hard time of it, but I am now able to walk out in town. My health is improving fast. I expect to go to my regiment next week (if I keep improving as I have been), which is in Nashville, Tenn. ((pg.2)) There are more soldiers dies of disease, than are killed in the battle field. I have been in the hospital here in Danville, (either sick or well) for the last two months, and it is distrefsing(sic) to see the soldiers dying daily. there has over three hundred soldiers died in this place, since I have been here. We have had as many as three dead men in this house at once. Sometimes their wives come to see them, or their brothers, or fathers, and it looks hard to see their friends die, and no person to weep with them, or share their sorrow, or speak a word of comfort to them. Sometimes they bury them here, and sometimes they take the body home.
((pg.3)) I knew one case in which a father came to see his son, who was sick, and the son got well, and the father

took sick and died. and another case in which a woman came to see her husband. the man got well, and his wife took sick and died. and I have heard of a good many other similar circumstances. These things appear to be lamentable, but we should be satified with our lot, let it be cast where it may. We have no right to complain, because every complaint we make is against our Supreme Ruler. As for my part, (as you know I always am) I am perfectly happy and contented. It is true I ((pg.4)) had a pretty hard time of it, when I was sick, amd some of them thought I was going to wink out, but I was not the least discouraged, or home-sick. I feel thankful that I am alive, and that my health is as good as it is. I expect that you have heard from brother David since I have. I have not heard from him since he left here. (Remember, they were basically traveling together in the war.) Hoping that these few lines may find you all in good health, I will close by asking you to write immediately. I don't ask it because it is fashionable, but because I want you to write. Direct to (I havn't (sic) got room) yours respfly, J.J. Huffman (all sic)

Enclosed, please find five dollars "((written on the upper border, upside down))

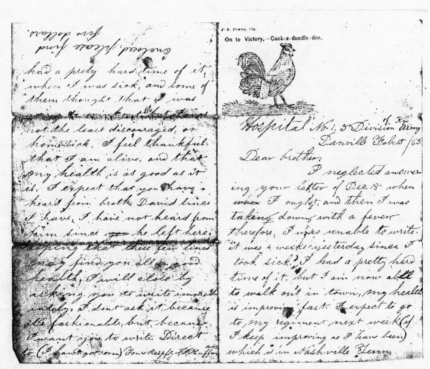

LTR4a

There are more soldiers dies of disease, than are killed in the battle field. I have been in the hospitals, here in Danville (either sick or well) for the last two months. and it is distressing to see the soldiers dying daily, there has over three hundred soldiers died in this place, since I have been here. we have had as many as three dead men in this house at once. Sometimes their wives come to see them or their brothers, or Fathers. and it looks hard to see their friends die. and no person to weep with them, or share their sorrow, or speak a word of comfort to them. Sometimes they bury them here. and sometimes they take the body home.

I knew one case in which a father came up to see his son who was sick, and the son got well, and the father took sick and died. and another one in which a woman came to see her husband. the man got well, and his wife took sick and died, and I have heard of a good many other similar circumstances. These things appear to be lamentable, but we should not lament. we should be satisfyed with our lot; let it be the cast where it may. we have no right to complain, because every complaint we make, is against our Supreme Ruler. As for my part (as you know I always aim) I am perfectly happy and contented. it is true I

LTR4b

NOTES: (Letter 4)

Notice the near-perfect word usage, and, even, punctuation. Proper etiquette and manners are prevalant through his letters. Notice his compassion and feeling for the men lost, and their families, and the resoluteness of his comments and his belief in God. His description of his character traits are self-analyses to which he tried to stay true. His thankfulness to be alive is obvious. His comment about folks thinking he was going to "WINK OUT" was rather triumphantly stated, and striking in its "modern" tone. He never says what he was sick with, nor the diseases he might have seen around him in the hospital. (Is he again trying to protect his parents from these scenes?)

His comment that, "There are more soldiers dies of disease, than are killed in the battle field," is telling of the conditions around him in the camps, and even the hospitals. Grim thought for a young fellow fresh out of his family surroundings.

John J.'s travel with the 85th Indiana Volunteer Infantry subsequently has been active, and takes him through the central region.

After 8 months he proceeds down into the Chattanooga, Tennessee and Georgia areas.

Letter 5

His letter, of Sep 19-20, (1863) ((during the Battle of Chickamauga, located in Tenn and GA)), states:

"J.J.Huffman to Ann"

"Your kind favor came to hand yesterday and rec'd a earty (sic) welcome. I wasvary (sic) glad to hear that you was all well, especially that Sister (in-law) (sic) Matilda was recovering from her illness, for she writes me more lettters than any of you when she is well. You say if I get sick, and want any person to wait on me just let you know and you will be on horses. I would say in reply, that you can no more come here than you can go to heaven in a hand basket. ((and we thought that was a modern expression!)).

((pg.2)) Right now that battle is going on, and has been for some time. Bragg while fleeing before Rosecrans got vary (sic) heavely (sic) reenforced (sic) it is supposed, by Johnson (sic) and Lee both, and they turned ((the effect of the battle)), and one of the awfulest (sic) battles is being fought, that ever was known in an open field fight. Unfortunately for us, (or perhaps fortunately) (sic, as written) we are in the reserve corps, and do not have the honor of participating ((written above the line)) in the fight. our boys are vary (sic) anxious to go forward. We have no particulars of the fight. Our lofs (sic) is vary (sic) heavy . . . ."

(This excerpt is only a single two-sided page which may be part of another letter, and was originally un-identified as to author, or addressee. We have determined the author and addressee due to the similarity to many of the other letters, and references to family members.)

NOTES:(Letter 5)

IMPORTANT: His closeness to the commanding officers of this unit makes his statement of the severity of the battle at Chickamauga, GA. very interesting, in that he refers to the battle at a "timely moment" during the battle itself. He states it as: ". . . and one of the awfulest battles is being fought, that ever was known in an open field fight", with essentially the same words used in memoirs in the 1880's, but at the time when the story was fresh and new and still happening (in history). Remember that communications at this time were basically "word-of-mouth", and the report of such information was truly, "Garbage-in, garbage out." This may be one of the FIRST, and MOST-NEARLY CORRECT, renditions of the many later-recorded statements of the battle, that have later been quoted by most sources!! He was in a place where he could likely have heard the reports directly! His letter predates Sherman's Memoirs by about 12 years!

His additional comment to his sister when she offers to take care of him if he is sick, "You can no more come here than you can go to heaven in a hand basket" is delightful, since I thought that to have been a much more recent saying than it obviously was.

favor came to hand yes-
terstay, and keek a harty
welcome. I was very glad
to hear that you was
all well, especially that
Sister (in-law) Matilda was
recovering from her illness,
for she writes me more
letters than any of the
when there is well. You
say if I get sick, and
want any person to wait on
me just let you know and
you will be on hands.
I would say in reply that
you can no more come here,
than you can go to heaven
in a hand basket.

LTR5a

LTR5b

Letter 6

The next letter is from J.J.'s brother, David, on November 20th, 1863 to their sister Ann. He is in central Tennessee, at Fosterville, near Nashville.

He goes through the formalities they all use when writing a letter, and goes on to say: "I have nothing new to write so I will tell you the old tale. We are in camp at Fosterville. We have been here two weeks longer than we staid (sic) at one place for some time. We may remain here for a while if the Rebs stays ot (sic, for 'out') of Tenn. But if they make a raid we will have to travel again to keep them from destroying the railroad. We are fixed for living here if we remain We have homes built with chimneys to them and are living at the top of the pot. There has not any snow fell yet. It has rained considerable the last month but the weather has been very pleasant for this season of the year. Evrything (sic) appears to be quite calm at present The army appears to be lying Still. There is always a calm before a storm. So look out for news. ((Pg.2)) We have plenty of hard tack, Coffee, Sugar, beans and Sow belly to eat so there is no danger of us starving. I should not be surprised if we had a mefs (sic, for "mess") of fresh pork once in a while and a chicken for breakfast on Sunday morning as long as there is anything in Tenn. the soldiers will live well. It is raining very hard and they are bringing in clothing for the Soldiers so I will close Brother John and I are both well and I hope these few lines will find you all well.

I will close hoping to hear from you Soon.
Yours truly
D.L. Huffman
Co. J 85th Regt
Ind. Vol. Inft.
via Nashville Tenn"

NOTES: (Letter 6)

David is descriptive, but although he doesn't write very often himself, he cajoles the others to write to him.

His hopes of having a smooth winter, and good food with "top of the pot" living is a fond dream at this time and we don't know for certain whether it came to pass, or not. His story of the life of the soldiers is satisfying, and comforting to the folks back home. Is this part of his purpose??

Ladies at home continue to send letters back and forth to each other and to keep each other well-informed of the condition of their part of the family and community. They had a rather well-established mail routine that took the place of the 150 year-later Twitter and Facebook Media! Without telephones, etc, they must have felt somewhat stifled except through use of the mails, which were, themselves, not always well-developed everywhere.

Fosterville Tenn Nov 20th /63,
Miss E.A. Huffman
Dear Sister

I seat myself this
rainy evening for the purpose of addressing
you with a few lines in answer to
your kind epistle which I received a few
days since. I have nothing new to write
so I will tell you the old tale, We are
in camp at Fosterville, We have been here
two weeks longer than we have staid at
one place for some time, We may remain
here for a while if the rebs stays ot of
Tenn. But if they make a raid we will
have to travel again to keep them from
destroying the railroad, We are fixed for
[?] here if we remain we have
houses built with chimneys to them
and are living at the top of the pot,
There has not any snow fell yet, there
it has rained considerable the last month
but the weather has been very pleasant
for this season of the year Everything
appears to be quite calm at present the
army appears to be lying still, There is always
a calm before a storm, So look out for news.

LTR6a

We have p[...] [...] [...] Coffee
Sugar B[...] [...] jelly to eat
so there [...] [...] of [...],
I should [...] [...]prised if we had
a [...] mess of fresh pork once in a while
and a chicken for breakfast on Sunday
morning as long as there is anything
in them, the Soldiers will live well
It is raining very hard and they are
bringing in clothing for the Soldiers
so I will close Brother John & I are
both well and I hope these few lines
will find you all well
I will close hoping to hear from
you soon   yours truly
[signature]
[...]
New [...]ville

LTR6b

This letter is from Catharine McCreery, Ann's cousin. She is a fountain of information on all the local folks, and relates all the tribulations that the entire community is suffering, and the latest news on the soldiers as soon as she hears it.

Letter 7

Letter Catharine McCreery to Ann Huffman

"Liberty T (sic, for twp)
Hardin Co Ohio March the 14th, 1864

Dear Cousin it is with pleasure that I embrace the present opportunity of informing you of our wellfare (sic) we are all well at present and I hope these few lines may find you enjoying the same blefsing (sic) I received your letter and was glad to hear from you we are still living on uncle John Shusters place but we expect to move on our own next week. Now I will give you the descriptions of it. it is ½ quarter and it lays 2 miles north west of fathers it has 2 cabins on it 2 corn cribs and a wagon shed and a stable and 6 apple trees big enough to bear right smart fruit it has 37 acres cleared on it and it is all in clover and timothy would do to mow this summer the cleared land is entirely clear of stumps and trees it would mow with the mowing machine and it has a good sugar camp on it it is all nice rolling land it is rolling enough to build a bank barn on it ((a bank barn is one that has an entry for animals on the lower level and wagons and machinery on the second level)) and we pay $1200 for it there is land on two sides of it that can be bought well ann that is all about that only I should like to have you to come over and help us move the relations are all well here except Mary Whites youngest child it took the dyptheria(sic) last December it has been sick all winter and is not well yet and aunt Elizabeth Shuster has been very bad with the lung fever but is now getting better

George Shuster died in January he was only sick 5 days brother ebenezer buried his child about 3 week ago it was only sick 3 or 4 days the Dr said its sickness was inflamation of the lungs and the intermitting fever with it there is not much sickness in the country now there is one family has the small pocks (sic, pox) within 6 miles of us I must tell you Elihue Shuster (pg.2)

Samuel Tressel George Tressel and John Wells and two of the Levi Larues boys that is Sarah Shusters husband have all enlisted and gone to the army and lots of others their (sic) is great excitement here about the draft well ann these little girls of ours says they would like to have you fetch another kiss over for them yourself write and tell us whither (sic) C.W.Strawns house was burnt or not as we heard it lately but did not know whither it was so or not and if it is so write and let us know how it got burnt and whither they got their things out of it or not and where they are living now tell us whither your mother can walk any better or not I want you to write all the particulars and whither the neighbor boys are living and well yet that went to the army except Thomas Davy William has give up coming in there till next fall I think by that time you can come out here with him and pay us a visit tell Finly to come out here and take easter with us tell him that their (sic) is lots of girls out here and they are just more than a getting married

their (sic) has been near a dozen wedding (sic) within 2 months some married their men when they were home on furlough and I guess I must quit for fear you cant read what I have got wrote (sic) give my love to all the relations and neighbors so nothing more at present still remaining your till death write soon

Catharine McCreery to ann huffman"

(Following is a section written by the mother for her son to his cousin but definitely written in the mother's handwriting.)

"well Martin I send My love to you I went to school all winter Our school was out last week I have gained the prize at every school that I have went (sic) to since I have been in Hardin County my teacher last winter give me a pocket bible with gilted edge and clasps to it Cost 6o cts so nothing more at present

Luther Melanethon McCreery to Martyn (sic) Luther Huffman &c"

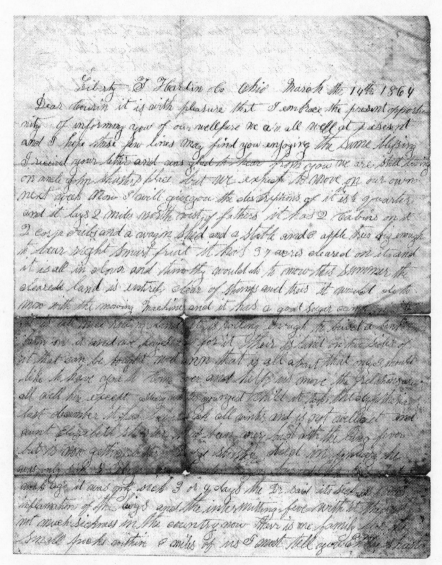

LTR 7a

...Wetzel George Foster and John Hills and two of Levi Leavers boys ... Shusters husband have all enlisted and gone to the ... and lots of others their is great excitement here about the draft well ann this little girl of ours says they would like to have you to fetch another kiss over for them yourself write and tell us whither H. W. Sitzmans house was burnt or not as we heard it lately but did not know whither it was so or not and if it is so write and let us know how it got burnt and whither they got their things out of it or not and where they are living now tell us whither your mother can walk any better or not I want you to write all the particulars and whither the neighbor boys are all living and well yet that went to the army except thomas Eary. William we give up coming in this fall next fall I think by that time you can come out with him and they as to visit tell Foot to come out here and take easter with us tell him that their is lots of girls out here and they are just more than getting married their Has been near a dozen wedding within 3 months some married there when auhto they were home on furlough well I guess I must quit for fear you cant read what I have got wrote give my love to all the relatives and neighbors so nothing more at present still remaining yours till death write soon

Catharine Wolbery to ann Wippman

well Martin I send my love to you I went to School all winter our School was out last week I have gained the prize at our School that I have went to since I have been in ... County my teacher last winter give me a pocket bible with gilted edge and clasps to it cost 60 cts so nothing more at present

Father Melancthon Wolbery to Martin Luther Hoffman &c

LTR 7b

NOTES: (Letter 7)

J.W. Kimmel, while a "community" friend of the Huffmans who obviously knew them for a long time before going into the service, lived in Tuscarawas's neighboring Carroll County, and had enlisted there into the 51st Ohio Vol. Inf., which took him on a different tour throughout the War.

The 51 st OVI was on duty in Ky, until Feb 1862; took an expedition on the Ohio River to reinforce Gen. Grant, then on to Nashville, Tenn. They occupied Nashville, through July 9, 1862 when they were moved to Tullahoma, Tenn, to join Nelson's division. They marched to Louisville, KY, in pursuit of Bragg Aug 21-Oct 22, 1862, having been involved in the battle of Perryville on Oct. 8, and continued to Nashville, through Nov 7, with action at Dobbins Ferry, near Laurence, on Dec 9, advanced on Murphreesboro, Tenn, Dec 26-30, and battle at Stones River on Dec 30-31, 1862 and Jan 1-3, 1863.

They were on duty, at Murphreesboro until June 63, in the Tullahoma Campaign June 23-July 7; in McMinnville until Aug 16, crossing Cumberland Mountain, the Tennessee River, and into the Chickamauga Campaign, with the battle of Chickamauga on Sept 19-20. They were involved in the siege of Chattanooga from Sept 24-Nov 23, including the reopening of the Tennessee River, and on into the Chattanooga-Ringgold, Ga Campaign (Nov 23-27), with its battles of Lookout Mountain, Nov 23-24, and Missionary Ridge, Nov 25, Ringgold Gap, and Taylor's Ridge, Nov 27. They had duty at Whiteside until Jan. They then camped at Blue Springs Camp near Cleveland, Tenn, until May, 1864.

Letter 8

It was during this time that J.W.Kimmel wrote a letter, now missing from the collection, to Ann Huffman, along the following lines:

"We are in a valley high in the mountains of Eastern Tennessee. We don't know how much longer we will be here.

It is still quiet here and have not been any skirmishes or troop movements.

Some of the boys have corn ((perhaps a handful they had been given by their fathers as they left home)) and they are planting in hopes of having a few ears to eat before we move on. This early in the spring, we may have the opportunity to plant twice, God willing.

We have good water from a goodly number of natural springs and a large area to spread out into. Times are pretty good and we have plenty to eat."

NOTES: (Letter 8)

Blue Springs Camp is in a valley in Southeastern Tennessee alongside Blue Springs Ridge, just three miles outside Cleveland, and adjacent to the Georgia-Tennessee border. Just which side of the Blue Springs Ridge they are on is conjecture, but it seems they are separated from Lead Mine Valley, and the adjoining Lead Mine Ridge, by the Blue Springs Ridge to the west of Blue Springs Valley.

The two ridges, (from a map of the area by the TVA), are listed as the highest ridges in the area. Their summits together form the line of the Eastern Tennessee Natural Continental Divide, where the water from the western side flows to the Gulf Coast, and the waters from the eastern side flow to the

Atlantic Ocean. This is the only major Continental Divide east of the Rockies.

The Continental Divide jumps from one of the ridges to the other as the range proceeds roughly northeast and southwest.

There was known to be an "active" lead mine in the southern-most end of Lead Mine Ridge at a pass where both a road and the railroad intersect to pass through Lead Mine Ridge, toward the west and on to Georgia.

The ridges (from my recollection) were about 3/8 of a mile apart and the summits about 350 feet above the broad, flat valleys. They offered good protection, both weather-wise, and militia-wise, even though they were high up in the mountains.

The general area of both valleys is near the Red Clay Prehistoric center of the Ancient Cherokee Nation. This suggests that the Union forces may have been guided there due to their close association with the Cherokee Indians, who were friendly, uncommonly educated, and who were capably used as guides and scouts by the Union throughout the War.

It is felt that the Union, in the location as it had here, could have observed Confederate troop movements up and down both sides of the "Divide" by sending observers to the tops of trees (or other prominences, naturally-occurring or man-made) to visually observe signs of troop movements, (dust, smoke, and tree-felling, etc).

Besides a fertile valley, large amounts of good water, (having 52 springs in the valley, even this high in the mountains), observation advantages, protection from weather and attack, as well as a lead mine to provide needed materiels, there was also a road and an intersecting railroad for convenience in moving troops and supplies into and out of the region. General Patton would have been pleased to have had such a good location for his troops in W W II.

It was during this period that Joseph W. Kimmel wrote to his friend, Eve Ann Huffman, back at home.

Letter 9

"Camp Blue Springs Tenn Apr 21 (1864)

Friend

It is with the greatest of pleasure that I take my seat this evening to answer your kind and most welcome Epistle which came to hand this morning and these fewleaves (sic) me well and I hope that when these few lines comes to they find you enjoying the best of health I have got 3 or 4 letters from Rose Township Ohio ((Ohio, scrunched into the space between lines)) Since I left The last one I got from there was about aweek (sic) ago from sister Maria They are all well Maria has got married since you and me (sic) left She is married to a young man by the name of Oliver Farber Turn over (pg.2)

She was married The next Sunday after We left and I Expect I will get aletter (all sic) from you before long and give the news that youhave (sic) married some of the Indiana boys but it don't make any difference about that for I think Every one or to (sic, for "ought to") marry when they please and who they please (extra loop on the last 'e', but not an extra letter)

I was glad to hear from ("from" written above the line as if left out) John and that he was well When you write again let me know how your brother David is getting along and where he is for I always like to hear from a soldier and when you write to David tell him I send my best respects to him I would like to see him him and me used to have a great deal of fun when we went to scool (sic) together at McKaskia School

House I got aletter (sic) from Thomas McKaskia (pg.3)A few days ago they were all well

well ann I must tell you how I am getting along I am getting along firstrate I like soldiering very well So far I would rather be here than at home as long as we have as good times as we have now We are in camp about 3 miles from a little town by the name of Cleveland It is a nice place here for a camp We Expect (sic) to stay here A little while but we dont know how long for the rebs are pretty close here and we dont know how soon they may attack us but I hope we will stay here for awhile I believe I have written you all the news for the present and I must quit for it is getting late so no more at present but I still remain Your Friend J.W.K."

"Direct your letter to Joseph W. Kimmel Camp
near Cleveland (last three words crossed off)
Camp near Cleveland Tennessee
51st Regt Co K OVI

(Pg.4)
Write as soon as this comes to hand and give me all the news Give my respects to Fidia"

"When this you see remember me (Encircled with a looping string of loops)
Though far apart we may be

From Your Friend, J.W.K.
To, his friend Eveann Huffman"

(Continual scroll of attached loops approximating a string of J's and capital S's)

(At bottom and VERY large)
"YOURS TRULY"

Camp Blue Springs Tenn Apr

Friend

Ann

It is with the greatest of
Pleasure that I take my seat
This Evening to answer your
kind and most welcome Epistle
Which came to hand this
morning and these few lines leaves
me well and I hope that
when these few lines comes to
they find you enjoying the
best of health I have got 3 or 4
letters from Rose Township Ohio since I
left the last one I got from
there was about a week ago from
Sister Maria they are all well
Maria has got married since
you and me left She is married
To a young man by the name
of Oliver Barber turn over

LTR 9a

She was married The next Sunday after We left and I Expect I will get a letter from you before long and give The news That you have married some of The Indiana boys but it dont make any difference about That for I Think Every one orte marry when They please and when They please I was glad to hear from John and That he was well When you write again let me know how your brother David is getting along and where he is for I always like to here from a Soldier and when you write to David tell him I send my best respects to him I would like to See him him and me used to have a great deal of fun when we went to School together at McKashea School House I got a letter From Thomas McKashea

A few days ago they were all well Well aun I must tell you how I am getting along I em getting along Cfirstrate I like Soldiering very well So far I would rather be here than at home as long as we have as good times as we have now We are in camp about 3 miles from a little town by the name of Cleveland It is a nice place here for a camp We expect to stay here A little while but we dont know how long for the rebs are pretty close here and we dont know how soon they may attack us but I hope we will stay here for awhile I believe I have written you all the news for the present and I must quit for it is getting late So no more at present but Still remain Your Friend J, W, K
Direct your letter To
Joseph W, Kimmel Camp Near Cleveland
Camp Neur Cleveland Tennese
J-14th Regt Co K O, V, I

LTR 9c

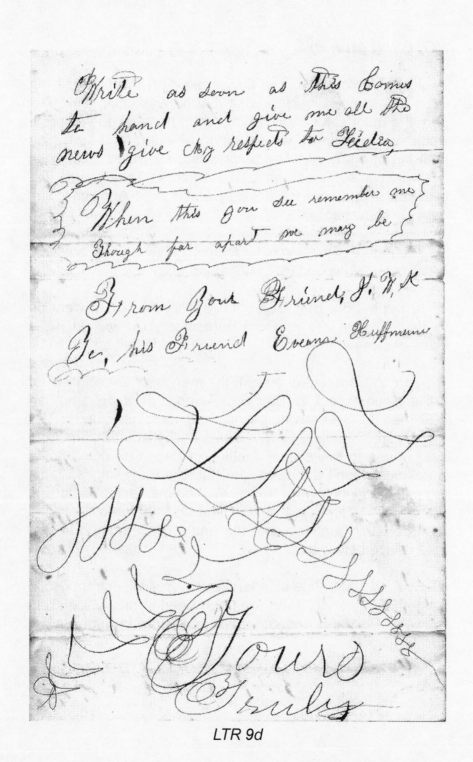

Write as soon as this comes to hand and give me all the news give my respects to Hester

When this you see remember me Though far apart we may be

From Your Friend, H, W, K

To, his Friend Evans Huffman

Yours Truly

LTR 9d

NOTES: (Letter 9)

Joseph's flourishing writing-strokes on the back of the letter look curious, but realizing that he was using a wet-ink pen, the point still contained ink when he finished writing. It was usual practice to write a string of letters and squiggles until the pen ran dry. The point was then wiped dry to use fresh next time. He emphasized the words, "Truly Yours", and included a poem, since he very much liked Ann, and was trying to show her that!!

The nature of what was happening in his area, is indicated in the notes of his unit (51st OVI) appended.

In Sept 1863, Brig Gen John S Williams (CSA) went up to Blue Springs, Tenn. Genl Burnsides (US) was at Bull's Gap—9 miles in front. On 10/10/63 Burnsides attacked.

Gen Williams had only 1700 men and 2 batteries of artillery and except for Brig Gen Alfred E Jackson, who had 500 men at Greeneville, Tenn, had no other support for more than 100 miles. Gen Williams multiplied campfires and beat drums to make an exhibition of forces he didn't have. Burnsides wasn't deceived, and attacked anyway. Williams retreated at night toward Bristol, Va., (on the Tenn / Va border) but he was intercepted at Hamilton and captured. Both the battle of Chickamauga and the battle of Chattanooga had taken place before this.

By April 1864 (date of letter) Feds were well entrenched in Eastern Tennessee. (The area had been somewhat divided between Northern and Southern sentiment throughout the War.)

Letter from J. J. Huffman to his sister E. A. Huffman. (Date undefined but somewhat prior to Apr 25, 1864)

Letter 10

In this letter, J.J. Huffman responds to his sister's supposed question regarding his thoughts on her proposed moving to Indiana "with" a man who had several children, and whose wife had died. The implied objective would have been to set up housekeeping for/with him in starting a homestead farm in Indiana.

J. J. says to her several admonitions along the following lines:

"You ask whether you should move to Indiana with (??)

Indiana is not as civilized as you have been accustomed to in Ohio. Times there are much harsher. Indian raids are still known to occur with fair frequency.

You will be alone from your family who are still there in Ohio, with mails not nearly as well-established.

Being a farm wife is more difficult and demanding than the town-life you are used to.

Remember, you are young and the man you are suggesting is nearly twice your age and has children almost as old as you are.

Remember, also, that if you were both to have a long and able life, there may not be a problem, but if he should die sooner than an old age, say 60, then you would still be a young woman with a farm in Indiana to maintain, and no family about.

God forbid he should pass even earlier, you might find yourself with the responsibility of a farm to maintain, and of "children who are not even of your own issue".

I suggest to you to think about these things and "if your mind follow your heart, you have my permission".

((She does not apparently move to Indiana with this man, but goes later with her extended family for a short period when they relocate there.))

The following letter was sent from J. J. Huffman to his sister, Ann, while on a march from Murphreesboro,Tenn, and bedding down for the night in Tullahoma, Tenn.

Letter 11

He writes:

"Tullahoma, Tenn
April 25th /64

Dear Sister:

Your kind epistle of no date, came to hand a few days since and was thankfully received and carefully perused. I was especially glad to hear that your health was good, and that you had a good home and was well satisfied. You will find that if you take a friend with you that you will always have friends.

Ever be ready to do a favor, and always have a kind word for every person; and above all, as virtue is the brightest jewel that ever a Lady was adorned with, adhere strictly to its principals (sic). My advise (sic) to you, not to go to Indiana, need not discourage you in the least; as you are already there; and well satisfied. I was only afraid you would be discontented. But I would advise you, not to go to Clay Co. unlefs (sic) Brother George moves out there, which I think extremely doubtful. We are now on a march and Have just camped out for the night, at Tullahoma Tenn, about 45 miles South of Nashville. We have been marching for the last six days. I cannot tell you where we will stop. I received your letter at Murphreesboro, while on the march, but could not avail myself of an opportunity to answer it, untill (sic) the present, which is a vary (sic)poor one. As you (sic) letter was not dated

I could not tell how long it was on the way. I hope you will write immediately.

We receive our mail, while marching. I hope you will remember me in your prayrs. (sic)

Your affectionate brother,
J. J. Huffman
85th Ind Vol
Via Nashville, Tenn

P.S. Brother David and I are both well; and Stand the march well.

J.J. H."

NOTES: (Letter 11)

He kindly reminds Ann, several times, to date her letters to help him know when they were written

She has somehow gotten to Indiana, (despite his warnings against Clay Co), and is already living there. We are not sure where she is staying, nor with whom.

He counsels her in the application of her virtue to her living, with some pretty eloquent advice.

He is strong in his Christian beliefs and has taken another opportunity to give Ann more big-brotherly advice.

This letter is just days before the start of the Atlanta Campaign (May-Sept).

Tullahoma Tenn. April 25" /64

Dear Sister,

Your kind Epistle of no date, came to hand a few days since, and was thankfully received, and carefully perused. I was especially glad to hear that your health was good, and that you had a good home and was well satisfied. You will find that if you take a friend with you, that you will always have friends. Ever be ready to do a favor, and always have a kind word for every person; and above all, as virtue is the brightest jewel that ever

LTR 11a

a Lady was adorned with,
adhere strictly to its
principals. My advise
to you, not to go to Indiana,
need not discourage. you in
the least; as you are already
there, and well satisfied.
I was only afraid you would
be discontented. But I would
advise you, not to go to
Clay Co unless Brother George
moves out there, which I
think extremely doubtful.
We are now on a march and
have just camped for the
night, at Tullahoma Tenn.
about 75 miles South of
Nashville. We have been
marching for the last six
days. I cannot tell you
where we will stop. I
received your letter at

Murfreesboro, while in the
march, but could not
avail myself of an opportunity. to answer it, untill
the present, which is a very
poor one. As you letter was
not dated I could not
tell how long it was on
the way. I hope you will
write immediately. We receive
our mail, while marching.
I hope you will remember
me in your prays.
Your affe-
ctionate brother,
L. A. Huffman
85 Ind vol
Via. Nashville
Tenn.

P. S. Brother David and I, are
both well; and stand.
the march well.

LTR 11b

The next letter, from J. J. Huffman to his sister Ann, comes from Kingston, Ga., apparently participating in the battles on the Atlanta Campaign, since the battle at Kingston was May 18-19, and his letter was written on the 22nd. The battles at Resaca, Kingston, Cassville, and advance on Dallas, had already taken place by this time. They are involved in the frequent skirmishes.

Letter 12

J. J. writes:

"May 22nd 1864

Dear Sister:

I received your kind letter day before yesterday, and was quite glad to hear from you, especially to hear that you was enjoying good health; and I hope, when these few lines reaches you, they will still find you enjoying the same blessing. Brother David and I are still blefsed (sic, for "blessed") with good health, but we have endured considerable hardship in the way of fighting, and marching, since last I wrote you. I will not pretend to describe to you, what we have done, for it would be uselefs; (sic, for "useless") besides, you will have it in the papers long before this reaches you. We're now in Georgia, near Kingston. We have halted here to wrest(sic) a day or two; and then we expect to resume our journey. Save yesterday, and to day, we have not been from under the sound of the Cannon, for the last two weeks. We have not done much vary (sic) hard fighting, but have been skirmishing considerable. The rebs are in full retreat, and it is unknown to us, where they will make the next stand. We belong to the Twentieth Corps commanded by Gen Hooker. This country looks vary (sic) desolate; more than half of the dwellings being evacuated. On the evening of the 19 th a portion of our Brigade made a charge on CassVill (sic), and took the place, the rebs leaving in confusion.

Our soldiers feasted sumtuously (sic), on suppers prepared for the rebs; besides, bacon, tobacco, sugar, and molasses; which come in vary good play (sic); for our boy was hungry and tired. We expect to leave this place tomorrow, but I dont know where we will go. You ask my advise (sic) about going with the family you now live with; I will give you none; do as you think best. Please write soon.

Your affectionate Brother,

J.J.Huffman
Co J, 85th Regt Ind Vol.
2nd Brig 3rd Div 20th A.C.
Army of the Cumberland"

May 22" 1864

Dear Sister,

I received your
kind letter day before yesterday,
and was quite glad to hear from
you, especially to hear that you
was enjoying good health; and
hope, when these few lines
reaches you, they will still
find you enjoying the same
blessing. Brother David and
I, are still blessed with good
health, but we have endured
considerable hardships in the
way of fighting and marching,
since last I wrote you, I will
not pretend to describe to you,
what we have done; for it wants
be useless; besides, you will
have it in the papers long

LTR 12a

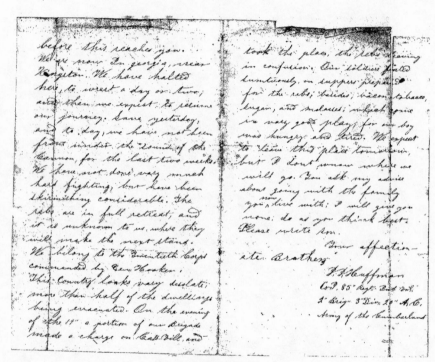

LTR 12b

NOTES: (Letter 12)

Kingston is in the northwest corner of Georgia not too far from Rome. It is between Chattanooga and Atlanta. Cassville is a town about five miles due east of Kingston.

The Huffmans are with Sherman's Army, in the 20 th Corps which occupied Atlanta.

Since the Huffmans are not given to easy complaining, we assume things must have been pretty terrible for those several weeks. J. J. has diligently gone out of his way to protect the family from the effects of those difficult scenes. He has instead focused his writing on the positive sides of the incidents.

Kingston, Ga, in Bartow County, Ga, was an important jointure of the Western and Atlantic Railroad, with a spur west to Rome, Ga, and served as a major hospital and supply location in the early years of the War. The first Confederate hospital was located there, in the Wayside Home. The soldiers wounded in the battles of Perryville, Chickamauga, Missionary Ridge and the Dalton-Kingston campaign were treated, and many died, there.

At the end of the war, Confederate Gen Wm Wofford surrendered his troops (of the last army east of the Mississippi River) there on May 12, 1865.

The epic story of the "General" locomotive, of the "Great Train Chase", involves Kingston Ga.

Letter 13

The following letter is from our relative, William Bowman, fighting with the 126th Ohio Volunteer Infantry, after he was taken prisoner on the second day's fight at the Battle of the Wilderness, on May 6th, 1864.

In the following month, he, and a great many of his fellow troops of the 126th, were moved from prison to prison, (Belle Island, and Florence, SC) until they arrived at Camp Sumter, in Georgia, a Confederate prison under the command of Captain Henri Wirz.

William wrote from Camp Sumter to his friend David Huffman:

"June the 2nd 1864
Camp Sumter georgia
((Presently known as "Andersonville Prison"))

Mr David Huffman
Dear friend

it is with pleasure that I seat my sealf (sic) this morning to let you know that I am well and hearty and to let you know that I am a prisioner(sic) I was captured on the evening of the sixth of May and they have used us midling (sic) well since we have been prisioners (sic) I was captured in the Wilderness close to the rapadan river (sic) on the second days fight I have not got anny (sic) thing more to write at the present sow (sic) I will close Good by

(Pg.2)

William Bowman
Prisioner(sic) of war"

NOTES: (Letter 13)

This letter, perhaps more than any of the others, is more interesting for what it DOESN'T (or CAN'T) SAY than for what it DOES SAY. William is very careful to say very sterile things about his experience in Camp Sumter. He says they "are well and hearty". If a prisoner would have COMPLAINED ABOUT ANYTHING in the camp, food, sanitation, or treatment, it is likely that the letter would NEVER have gotten out, or that the prisoner would have been beaten, or been the object of some severe sort of retaliation.

June the 2 1864

Camp Sumter georgia

Mr David Huffman

Dear friend

it is with pleasure that
I seat my self this morning
to let you know that I am
well and hearty and to
let you know that I am
a prisioner I was captured
on the evening of the
sixth of May and they
have used us nothing well
sine we have been prisioners
I was captured on the
wilderness close to the
rapadan river on the second
days fight I have not
got anny thing more
to write at the preasant
sow I will close good by

LTR 13a

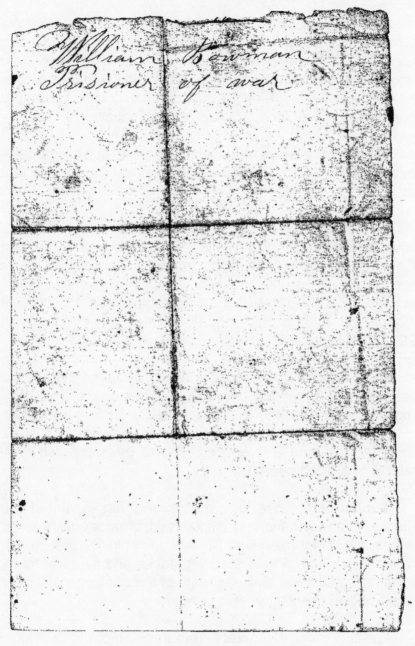

LTR 13b

NOTES on Background of Andersonville Prison:

Andersonville Prison is the modern name of the Civil War Confederate prison camp, Camp Sumter, in Southwestern Georgia. It was opened in Feb 1864, designed to accommodate 10,000 prisoners. At its closing it had housed 42,000 men with nearly 13,000 deaths, due to unsanitary conditions, lack of food, and lack of medical care.

From the time it was opened, the prison became overcrowded so fast that it was reported to be unable to feed the 8000 inmates and troops by March 31, 1864

At the time William, (and the many others of the 126th OVI who were captured at the Wilderness on May 6 th,) arrived, Camp Sumter was "packed to capacity", according to official reports, which was 10,000 men. (Some reports had capacity listed as 12,000) On May 8 th the report was 12, 213 with 728 deaths. By May 18 th, 18,000 inmates, and by May 20 th, 20,000 were present.

When William wrote from Camp Sumter (June 2 nd), it was listed as 24,000 inmates with 100 dying each day. In moving the prisoners from the Wilderness to Camp Sumter there is evidence that they had stayed for a very short time in a prison in South.Carolina (Florence, SC) and perhaps also Belle Island, near Richmond, VA.

William says, in effect, that everything is alright, but ignores that they have very limited food, of poor quality, mixed with inedible ingredients as fillers. The sanitation was so bad that the small creek was solid with feces and by accident the toilet area had been built upstream of the drinking water area. Disease and pestilence were rampant.

Typhoid fever, dysentery, gangrene, diphtheria, bilious fever, and numerous other maladies all occurred at the same time, without adequate medicine, or treatment. ((Inoculations were tried here for the first time to stem some of the diseases, with little success.)) The bad food, too, was indigestible and caused its share of deaths.

On July 8 th, the official report was that there were 30,000 being held, but the number was revised to 29, 400 on July 10 th. The highest number reported was on Aug 11 th, 1864; 33,000.

On Aug 13 th, there was a storm that washed away part of a wall and in so doing, a new natural spring opened up and supplemented the fresh water supply in the creek, in a place where it could be used. It was promptly named "Providence Spring"!! (Inmates had dug 200 wells with their bare hands by July 1, 64, in an effort to get fresh water, most of which had been futile attempts.)

There were several organized attempts to escape from the Camp, but only one person ever escaped through the tunnels A series of tunnels had been dug, including rather large rooms underground, but they were discovered and filled. Six ring leaders of a group of inmate "raiders" were tried by their own officers (Union), were hanged and buried dishonorably in the prison cemetery.

By April 28, '65, the last of the 12,912 inmates who died there had been buried. A Union inmate, Dorance Atwater, and Clara Barton, (nurse), worked diligently after the end of the War, to finalize the records of those who had died, enabling most of the families to recover the personal effects of the deceased, and to locate their burial sites.

What dedication that displayed!

That ended a horrendous chapter of warfare in the civilized world!

The prison commandant, Heinrich Hartman (Henri) Wirz, was hanged in the first war crimes trial in US history on Nov 11,1865, at the US Capitol Building to chants of "Remember Andersonville".

One of the Union Soldiers held in Camp Sumter was an accomplished sketch artist, who made pictures of troops and scenes around the compound to pass his time.

Several of the many inmates have attained a level of fame due to these pictures, which were shared and passed on by the other inmates as they communicated after their service was completed and they had been released from their detainment.

One set of these pictures was reproduced by a member of the 126 th OVI and was presented to the "Andersonville Prison" about 1922. The prison was being commemorated as a National Historic Site by the Department of Interior, for which they requested mementoes from survivors to enhance the "museum experience" of the proposed site restoration at that later time.

One of the most famous of the inmates pictured was a boy (truly not yet an adult), George Hillicks, by name, of Company L, 16 th Illinois Vol Cavalry. He, as most others, was given a uniform that fit him when he was inducted into the Army. In his case, however, this young, (perhaps even under-aged), fellow had not yet attained full-growth. In the next few months he grew to exceptional height. Before he was able to get a re-issue of his uniform, he was captured and brought to Camp Sumter. As he kept rapidly growing, he soon became the tallest inmate in the prison. Since, like the others, he was poorly fed, his growth-spurt left him very thin and somewhat gaunt. He soon became known throughout the camp as "Flagstaff", because of his resemblance to a flagpole, and nicknames not being very flattering at that time.

The artist depicted George as he truly appeared, clothes somewhat tattered and disheveled, sleeves and trousers shorter than they should have been on his stretched-out arms and frame, and his countenance, sallow, his appearance, unkempt. He really could have used a larger uniform!

In a very famous later publication by John McElroy about Andersonville Prison, called "This Was Andersonville", Flagstaff's picture was doctored to make him appear more gaunt, and skeleton-like, with badly torn and tattered trouser legs and shirt sleeves. George was depicted with thinner arms and legs proving that the author had used his biases and the underlying intent of his book to portray how bad conditions had been in Camp Sumter. He altered the picture to his purposes by revising the original. Little did he know that many copies of the original would be/were distributed to the other inmates years later. The author had taken the opportunity to change his resources, rather than let them stand on their own merits.

Events at Camp Sumter were tragic enough that the picture did not NEED to be altered to convey the message for the book, but reliably reporting the facts would have been enough.

I submit that the copy of the sketch that I have is more believable than that presented in the book. While the conditions in Camp Sumter were abominable, there is never a good excuse for any author to doctor the facts, and to revise his resources, to help prove his point. The side-by-side comparison can be made on the picture pairing included here.

The series of sketches I have, which were received by my relative as they were distributed in 1922, were sent to the prison, the Department of Interior, and his prison camp friends of the 126 th OVI, by Dr. H. J. Peters of Ragersville, Ohio, a corporal in Co. E, of the 126 th, and also an inmate at Sumter.

The copies of the original sketches have been in the annals of the Department of Interior and Andersonville Prison (Camp Sumter) since the restoration was opened.

All versions of the sketches that may have been reproduced from the Andersonville book are incorrect, and are now subject to correction.

I have, furthermore, other sketches (perhaps also available to Mr. McElroy) of persons and significant scenes in the prison done by the same artist. See these in the following views.

GEORGE HILLICKS
Co. L, 16th Ill. Cav.

"Flagstaff"

FROM CPL. H.J. PETERS
126TH OVI
(PRESENTED TO
ANDERSONVILLE PRISON
ABOUT 1922

IN BOOK:
"THIS WAS ANDERSONVILLE"
OPPOSITE pg. 127, CHAPTER XI

H. J. PETERS, M. D.

Corporal Company E
126th Reg't O. V. I.

CORPORAL H. J. PETERS

Bucked and Gagged by Henry Wirtz
at Andersonville Prison

*for 4 hours for accidentally
came to close to a death
line*

CORP. H. J. PETERS

Company E, 126th O. V. I.

HOW I WENT IN   HOW I CAME OUT   One of the Chain Gang

ANDERSONVILLE PRISON

As the troops dedicated their attentions to the war and the happenings at the front, the ladies at home were dealing with the daily rigors of family life back on the farm

As friend Ruth Davy says when she writes to Ann :

Letter 14

"New Cumberland Ohio
Monday June 6th AD 64

Dear Friend.

I seat myself this afternoon to write you a few lines in answer to your kind letter that came to hand about two weeks ago. I expect you began to think that I wasent agoing to answer a tall (all sic) but the reason I did not write was because I did not feel like it. I was not verry well. (sic) I had the toothache about three weeks and I had something like the scarlet rash. I was very sick with it Nearly ever body around here has had it, but I feel pretty nigh strait (sic) again, onily (sic) I am a little tired The rest of the family is well and the health of our neighborhood (Pg.2)

is verry (sic) good at the present. (Criss) (sic) and (Till) (sic) ((for Christine and Mathilda)) was here yesterday a little while and they were all well. We went up to Davids (sic) Huffman in the evening to prayer meeting and their (sic) was agreat (sic) many their (sic). The house was full, and we had averry (sic) good meeting. The girls and David takes it very hard about Billy sense (sic) the word came that he is missing The poor fellow. It is hard to tell whether he is taken prisoner or killed I received a letter from Wesley a few days ago He stated he came through the battle safe and was well when he wrote We had agreat(sic) many brave soldiers that fell in that battle They it(sic) say it was the hards (sic) battle that has bin.(sic) (Pg.3)

This is Wednesday evening and we are all well. I will try and finish my letter but I havent mutch (sic) time I want to take it to the office to night Their (sic) is alot (sic) of youngsters agoing (sic) up to town to a singing to night I wish you was here to go with us for we would have a good time They have singing their (sic) every wednesday night

I was at a big sewing last thursday at Mrs. Strawns their(sic) was just twenty four old women and girls all together took supper their (sic). We had a verry (sic) pleasant time of it

well I must bring my letter to a close for this time. Excuise (sic) me for not writing sooner. I will try and do better the next time (pg.4)

I wish I was out their (sic) with you I bet you that we would have a big time I often think of the times we ust (sic) to have when you lived at the Strawns

I must quit You must write as soon as this comes to hand and I will try and answer sooner. Excuise (sic) my bad writing for I am in a hairry (sic, for "hurry") Good by. Write soon

From a friend
Ruth J. Davy
Ann Huffman
I will send you a peace (sic) of my new dress"

NOTES: (Letter 14)

Ruth and Ann are nearly the same age and have been "out of their house" for a little while, and living with others who need their help

[Reference to William Bowman and to Wes Hoopingarner in the war. Casual reference to the "Scarlet Rash", which "everyone has had".]

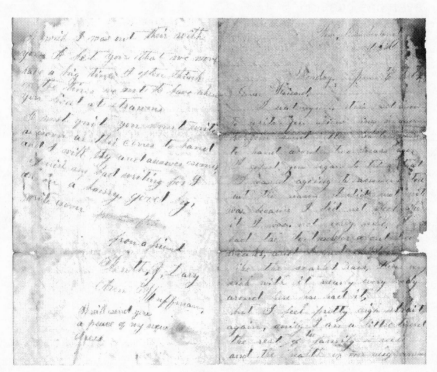

LTR14a

very good at the present!
(illegible) and (Lily) was here yesterday
a little while and they were all
well, we went up to David Ray
in the evening to prayer meeting
and their was a great many there
the house was full, and we had
a very good meeting.
the girls, and David, takes it
very hard about Billy, word
word came that he is missing
the poor fellow it is hard to
tell whether, he is taken
prisoner or killed

... a little girl Willy
... days ago he stated
... came through the battle
... and was well, when he wrote
... had a great many brave soldiers
that fell in that battle
they all say it was the hardest
battle that was in, ...

This is wednesday
and we are all well, I will
try and finish my letter
but I havent much time
I want to take it to the
office to night, their is a lot
of us youngsters going up to
town to a singing tonight
I wish you was here to go with
us for we would have a good
time they have singing there
every wednesday night

It was at a big meeting
thursday at the Stevens, there
was about twenty four old
women and girls all together
took supper, their we had a very
pleasant time of it
well I must bring my letter
to a close for this time, excuse
me for not writing sooner, I will
try and do better the next time

The next letter is the first one to Ann(e) from Mathilda, who is wife of Ann's brother, George, therefore her sister-in-law. She gives the most information on George, and is full of news. Her letter has writing on almost all the margins in her effort to get it all on the pages. She writes;

Letter 15

"New Cumberland Ohio July the 14th / 64

Miss Anne Huffman

dear sister

I rect your kind and welcomed letter indue time after it was wrote but have not answerd (sic) it for George was very sick when I got the letter so you will pardon me for not writing George had a hard spell of bilious fever ((vomiting until the stomach has nothing in it except bile, and then producing a fever that sometimes killed the patient)) he lay in the doctors hands for two weeks he was out of his head a part of the time it was a great pleasure [to me] (sic, written between the lines) that I could be with him in time of sickness and take care of him how many women are deprived of that priviliege (sic) their husbands are in far distant lands George is able to work again but not very stout yet our girls are almost big they are great company and help to me when their pa is gone for he is gone every day when he is able he is working for Dolvin again this summer he gets one dollar per day we have the prettiest and smartest and best children in our parts but not many of them as you know Mary went to school six mounths (sic) and only mist (sic) one day Maggy mist (sic) several days she was sick we have a good garden this summer our cabbage is a heading(sic) very nice we have plenty of beans and cucumbers we have a nice lot of sweet potatoes (pg.2)

You wanted to know something about the 126 reg—well I can't tell you much about them Bill Bowman is prisnor (sic) he is in the reb hands (poor Bill) Nick and Wes ((Hoopingarner brothers)) was well the last we heard poor Eli Barrick was shot in the head and his body burnt (sic) up (Oh, my)(sic) Lewis Beamer had his left arm shot off but he is getting along fine ((here a line is skipped and upside down in the space are the words, "Anne send me your photograph"))

I must begin again Pete Hoop (Hoopingarner) brought me a letter from brother John him and brother David was both well when he wrote the letter Pete got a letter from Wes I read it he was well and harty (sic) and Nick was well there is great excitement hear (sic) the report is the rebs is within six miles of the capital (sic) there is talk of a draft I fear I will haft (sic) to give up my husband O mercy what would I do old Aunt Polly Huffman has gone crazy about Bill some times she knows what she is doing but the (sic) most of the time she is raven (sic) she is an awful looking sight you wanted to know wether(sic) we were going to Clay Co.(Ind) next fall George says we are not going until the war is over and then we will go if our family is not to (sic) big I am willing to go where ever he goes and stay where ever he stays where ever he stays (repetition sic)

I will close write soon
your sister Mathilda Huffman "(Actually sister-in-law)

NOTES: (Letter 15)

The gruesome death of Eli Barrick occurred in the battle of the Wilderness in the early days of May 1864. In that battle the woods were set on fire by the cannon fire and many soldiers, including the helpless, and the wounded, were burned. William Bowman and Eli Barrick were both in the Wilderness at the same time, and Bowman was captured as prisoner of war, while Barrick perished (shot in the head, and his body burned up in the fire). William proceeded through several Confederate prison camps, down through S. C. and finally into Camp Sumter, in Georgia. A number of the 126th troops were captured at the same, and later, times, before ending up in Camp Sumter. (Andersonville Prison by its later, more famous, name.)

The margin notations are as follows; On the top margin of the front page "tell us how Michel Kimmels is getting along I am glad you got enough of 1 yd anyhow" On the reverse side in the top margin "mothers (sic) has a flax puting (sic) tomorrow afternoon I am going over to dance Mary and Magyn has knew (sic) sacks ((a dress made from cloth of flour sacks, that were preprinted by the sack maker, since so many flour sacks were being recycled for clothing)) They are going to send you a small bit of it". On the left margin on the reverse side, "write and send me your photograph now do".

The family of Hoopingarners are close friends of the Huffmans and others in the area. Wesley is captured and his story becomes better known in later letters in this collection.

New Cumberland Ohio July the 14

Miss Anne Huffman

dear sister

I rec't your kind and welcomed letter
in due time after it was wrote but
have not answered it for George was
very sick when I got the letter
you will pardon me for not writing
George had a hard spell of bilious
fever he lay in the doctors hands
for two weeks he was out of his head
a part of the time it was a great
pleasure to me that I could be with him
in time of sickness and take care of him
how many women are deprived of that
priviliege their husbands are in far
distant lands George is able to work
again but not very stout yet
our girls are almost big they are great
company and help to me when their
pa is gone for he is gone every
day when he is able he is a working
for Dolven again this summer he gets
one dollar per day we have the
prettiest and smartest and best children
in our parts but not many of them
as you know Mary went to school
six mounths and only mist one day
Maggy mist several days she was sick
we have a good garden this summer
our cabbage is a heading very nice we
have plenty of beans and cucumbers
we have a nice lot of sweet potatoes

LTR15a

You wanted to know something about the [ ] reg [ ] well I cant tell you much about them [ ] Bowman is prisnor he is in [ ] hand [ ] Bill [ ] Nick and [ ] was well the last we heard poor Eli Barick was shot in the head [ ] [ ] [ ] up [ ]

Seewis [ ] had [ ] arm shot off [ ] he is a getting along fine

I must begin again old Hoop [ ] brought me a letter from brother John him and father David was both well when he [ ] the letter Pete got a letter from Wes I read is he was well [ ] and Nick was well there is great excitement hear the report is th rebs is within six mils of the capitol there is talk of a draft I fear I will haft to give up my husband O mercy what would I do [ ] old aunt Polly Huffman has gone crazy about Will some times [ ] she knows what she is a doing but the most of the time she is raven she is an awful looking sight you wanted to know wether we were agoing to May [ ] next fall George says we are not agoing until the war is over and then I we will go if our family is not to big I am willing to go where ever he goes and stay while we he stays where ever he [ ] will close write soon your sister Matilda Huff[ ]

LTR15b

The following letter is from Ann's sister, Christine (Crissey), to bring her up-to-date on the affairs of the family. Ann seems to be "away" so that a letter is necessary to communicate with her.

Letter 16

"New Cumberland Ohio
Aug the 5th, 64

Mifs Ann (sic, for "Miss")

I once more more(sic) avail myself of th (sic) oportunity (sic) of writing you a few lines in answer to your letter which I recd some time ago but I am ashamed that I have not written before this time but I will try and do better hereafter We are all well at present and I hope when these few lines comes (sic) to hand they will find you the same We have very nice weather here at present We have had several very hard rains here for the last week and it hascooled of (sic) the air (pg.2)

Aunt Polly Huffman is laying sick again and we have to go down there and sit up with her and we have to be out in the harvest field Mathilda was working (away) from home about eight weeks but she came home day before yesterday They wanted her all summer but she would not stay she was working for George Reineharts He was married to Harriet Walls She has a baby about three months old and she has not been able to (sic) do anything ever since it was born Mifses (sic, for "Misses" or "Mrs") Strawn has a young son It is about three weeks old Ann Daivy (sic) is doing her work She wanted one of us but we could not go (pg.3).

Ann Tressel has a young daughter She calls it Mary Jane Mary Tressel is doing her work I suppose you heard that Sarah had a young son but it was dead Noah Fry was throwed (sic) off a beast and hurt very bad his father sent him to Waynesburg to carry a cradle home on a colt and when he got on it jumped and threw him off and broke his arm and hurt him severely It drug him through town by one foot

Henry Dilly has come home from the army He was wounded in the hand He saw our John before he come (sic) home He happened to go where they was (sic) You wanted to know in your other letter whether we found your pocketbook or not We did not find it (Pg.4)

George got a letter from John last week and they was well I have nothing more to write this time so I will close by wishing you good health Write your sister

C. J. Huffman"

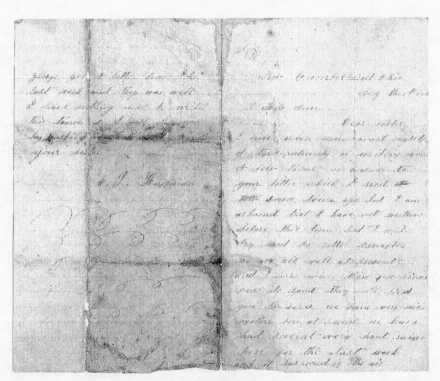

LTR16a

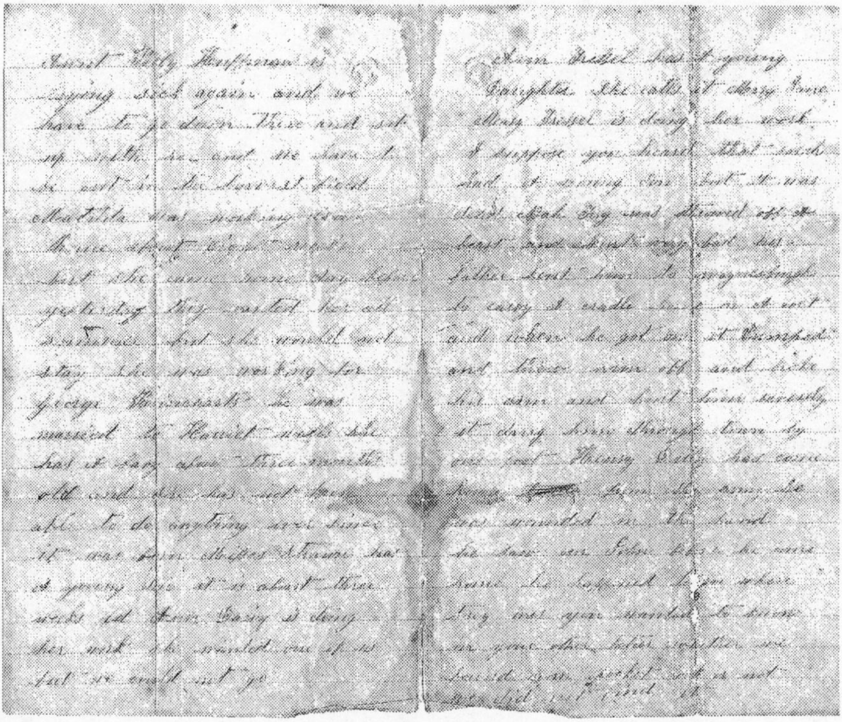

LTR16b

By this time in the war, J.J.Huffman, with the 85th Ind Vol Inf, has been transferred into the Ambulance Corps, accompanying Sherman's troops on the Atlanta Campaign, and is part of the famous 20th Corps, which was the primary group that conquered and besieged Atlanta, and later went on to the coast.

He relates some of the details to Ann after the fall of Atlanta, without apologizing for the delay in writing to her during the heat of the battles. We have no record of his experiences in the Ambulance Corp, except for his observations of the happenings.

Letter 17

He writes

"Atlanta Ga Sept 11th / 64

Dear sister

Your kind letter of the 14th (the following word seems to be "ultimo") is at hand. I was very glad to hear that you was well and well satisfyed (sic). I hope you will do well. Brother David and I are both blessed with good health. You will already have heard that Atlanta has fallen. Gen. Sherman moved his army in the rear of Atlanta, and cut the R.R. This is what might be called one of Sherman's brilliant flank movements. He entirely destroyed Hoods communications (Pg.2)

and greatly surprised him. Hood endeavored to cut his way through our lines, but finding that impossible, he got out the best way he could. In getting out Sherman cut his army in two, and completely routed him. The rebs left Atlanta in utter confusion. We killed, wounded and captured agood many of them. The northern part of Atlanta is entirely ruined. There is hardly a house in that part of the city, but what is riddled with our cannon balls. There was several women and children killed and wounded. The sitizens (sic) dug holes in the ground to live in to keep from being killed with our shells. Gen. Sherman notified Gen. Hood (pg.3)

that he was going to shell the city and requested him to remove the women and children, but he refused to do it and did not even inform them of Shermans (sic) intention. There are a good number of women and children in the city, but vary (sic) few men who are able to bear arms, and they got away from the rebs in the skedaddle. All citizens have to leave the city. All the families whose male representatives are in the Confederate Army or gone South are required to go South. The others can go north or south as they like.

This part of the army is completely whiped (sic), and I think this rebellion will play out in lefs (sic) than twelve months. It may be that the Indiana soldiers will come home to vote this fall. (Pg.4)

I will close: Hoping these few lines will find you blefsed (sic) with good health and trusting in God for his grace.

Your affectionate brother
J. J. Huffman

Address   Ambulance Corps 2ⁿᵈ Brig. 3ʳᵈ Div. 20 A.C.
Atlanta, Ga."

NOTES (Letter 17)

Not very "homey", and no preaching to his sister this time. Very direct and succinct as to what had happened and why. He was not apologetic for the women and children having been involved as they were, because he was quite certain they had been given a chance (through Gen Hood) to avoid the fighting. He was direct in blaming Hood for the consequences, when Hood had not warned the citizenry, of the impending fight as he had been asked to do. His disgust for Gen. Hood's lack of action to allow them to save themselves is obvious. So much for Southern chivalry and honor.

John J.'s verbal description of the remains of the city and the turmoil depicted among the citizens as they tried to avoid the fighting and fled the city is reminiscent of the scenes we all saw during the movie, "*Gone With the Wind*". It is a letter that renews the pangs of our intellect on reading this timely account to his sister back home.

He concentrates on the tactics of the Generals in this note rather than the life of a private soldier.

He feels pride, not only in defeating the Confederates, but also in out maneuvering them, yet does not brag nor boast of the feat. His relating of the outcome for the citizens, depending upon their individual allegiances is matter-of-fact and straightforward.

His feeling that the "rebellion will play out in less than 12 months" proves to be correct. He still refers to it as a "rebellion", as does President Lincoln.

It was obvious that voting is important to John and his Indiana friends, since he repeats that hope in several of his letters. The feeling of patriotism is evident.

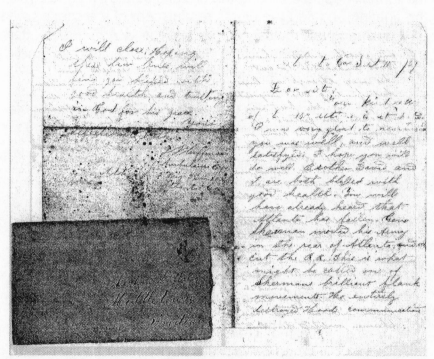

LTR17a

and greatly surprised him.
Hood endeavored to cut
his way through our lines,
but finding that impossible,
he got out the best way
he could. On getting out
Sherman cut his army in
two and completely routed him.
The rebs left Atlanta in
utter confusion. He killed, wounded, and captured a good
many of them. The Northern
part of Atlanta is entirely ruined.
There is hardly a house in that
part of the city, but what is
riddled with our cannon balls.
There was several women and child-
killed and wounded. The citizens
dug holes in the ground to
live in to keep from being
killed with our shells. Gen.
Sherman notified Gen. Hood,

that he was going to shell
the city, and requested him
to remove the women and children,
but he refused to do it, and did
not even inform them of Shermans intention. There are a good
many women and children in the
city that ... are
all ... bear arms, and they
got away from the rebs in the
skidaddle. The citizens have
to leave the city. All families
whose male representatives are in
the Confederate army, or gone
south, are required to go south.
The others can go North or South
as they like. This part of the
army is completely whipped and
I think this rebellion will
play out in less than a few
months. It may be that
the Indiana soldiers will
come home to vote this fall.

LTR17b

Letter 18

This letter was from Mathilda Huffman, (George Huffman's wife), to her sister-in-law, Ann.

"New Cumberland O Sept the 28 1864

Kind sister ((in-law))

I will try and write you a few (sic) lines in answer to your kind and most welcomed letter which I recd four weeks ago and was glad to hear from you but was very busy and neglected to write ontil (sic) now

I am entirely alone I will chat with you a little wile (sic) for company I came from Peter Hoops ((Hoopingarner)) this morning they have had a very cerious (sic) time doubtless you have heard (pg.2)

of their sickness so I will just tell you that the babe four weeks old will not live till knight (sic) Seys ((Cecil)) is a little better but not out of danger Maryon ((Marion)) was very bad both doctors gave him up but he got better but is worse agian (sic) Pete is well but his father is very poorly your mother has got better we are all well George is a working at B Manguns house he offered to go as a substitute ((to serve in the army as a substitute for another man who is called to go)) I fear he will go he gave twenty five (pg.3)

dollars to clear our own tp (for, "township") of a draft and now will go for rose (Rose Township) (((Big irony))) big Charley Scott is drafted and bob (sic) jim herre (sic) Their (sic) was fifty too (sic) drafted out of rose I will close and go to Hoops for they need me do not do as I done but write soon and I will try and do better next time

Mathilda Huffman"

"I closed my letter yesterday but I will write a few lines this morning and tell you (Pg.4)

Petes babe died last knight (sic) Its buried today they meet at the house at one oclock (sic) One more saint in glory Oh that I could have went at its age but Gods will be done

a word for our little girls

dear aunt ((Mathilda writes this as if her girls are speaking)) We often think and talk about you but cant (sic) see you but we got the patches of your dress and think it pretty we are a going to send you patches of our dresses the spoted (sic) is of the skirts and the plain of the waists goodby aunty

Mary and Maggie Huffman

(Written upside down on top of pg.3)
our little girls are all most big and the best looking in our township one favors their mother and the other their auntie Anne

(Written upside down on top of pg.2)
please write soon and I will answer"

NOTES: (Letter 18)

Mathilda again praises her little girls as being the prettiest in the township (They must be pretty cute or Mathilda wouldn't be able to get away with saying that all the time!!)

Besides apologizing for ignoring the need to write for so long, she relates the condition of the 'neighbors' and the family. Re-emphasized the facts of disease and death among them.

Mathilda again expresses her fears that her husband George will have to go into the draft, leaving her alone, even though he has cleared the township of the draft by paying money to the government! She is very fearful that he will have to go to war!!

She notes that George will have to go for another township in the wartime draft even though he cleared his own township's draft by paying money. She approaches "frantic" as she relates these problems!! There are apparently not enough men to fill the needs of the military in this area and they have implemented a severe draft situation, and she is terrified he will have to leave her.

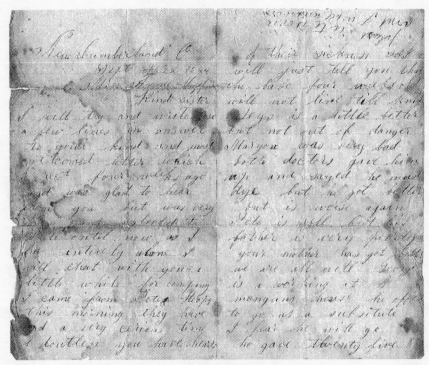

LTR18a

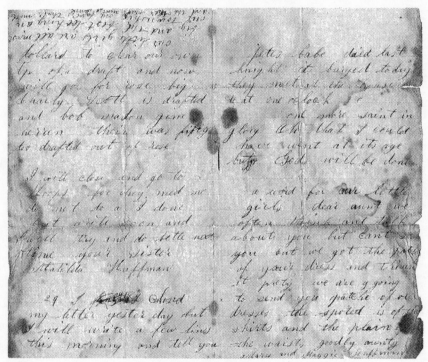

LTR18b

Letter 19

J.W.Kimmel, member of the 51st Ohio Vol Inf., finds himself in Gaylesville, Alabama, about 1 ½ months after the Battle of Atlanta and shortly before Sherman started his plundering March to the Sea (Nov. 14).

He writes:

"Camp of the 51st O.V.V.I. (sic)

Gailsville Alabama Oct 26 / 64

It is with the greatest of pleasure that I take my pen in hand to write you a few lines to let you know that I am well and hope these few lines find you enjoying good health I received your letter a few days ago and was glad to hear from you I don't know that I have anything of importance to write at this time we have been after the Johnnies (pg.2)

again for the last 3 weeks and have stopped here to rest for a few days I am out on picket about 8 miles from the Regt (sic) at bridge and we have pretty good times plenty to eat and drink i have got 2 or 3 letters from Rose Township in the last 2 or 3 weeks they are all well as a genewral (sic) thing i suppose you have heard who was drafted in Rose if you havenot (sic) it is no use for me to try to tell you for there is to (sic) many there is 52 drafted out of the township my to (sic) brothers was both drafted i got letters from cousin daniel (sic) Kimmel the other day tell Mary he was well but I am tired of writing this is the third letter I have wrote this morning i just finished one to George Strawn a few minutes ago i got a letter from him a few days ago he said they (pg.3) were all well he stated that they were making molassis (sic) and had lots of fun but I don't think they had as much fun as they had last fall when you and me was there but I will close for the mail is going out in a few minutes

To memories??? but still remain

J.W. Kimmel
To Annie Huffman"

NOTES: (Letter 19)

Atlanta fell Sept 2 in siege after the Battle of Atlanta, July 22, 1864.

The 51st under Gen Thomas, along with Sherman, proceeded to follow Gen Hood, whose troops were attempting to cut off the railroad from Chattanooga. The CSA were in Gaylesville, Alabama, on October 15, went to Gadsden on the 17th and over to Florence and Tuscumbia. Sherman followed as far as Gaylesville. ((This is how Kimmel happens to be in Gaylesville for this letter.)) From there, Sherman sent Gen Schofield toward Knoxville and Gen Thomas to Nashville. (Both later joined up to defeat Hood at Murphreesboro, Franklin and Nashville.) Joseph wrote this letter on 10/26 on picket duty near Gaylesville. ((or as Kimmel calls it, Gailsville)), Alabama.

There is a commemorative tablet in Gaylesville, which (in 11/1991) contained only a dozen house surrounding farms, and a centralized High School of perhaps 250 students, a derelict gas station/general-store/grocery. Although the town is on the only CONVENIENT route from Atlanta to Huntsville, the town had not-yet developed and (in 1985) was noted by a four-way stopsign intersection. ((P.P.S. When I was through there in 11/91, the town had a straight-through one direction, and stopped the other.))

In 2013, the school has become about 400 strong, and supports an active sports program, as well as strong academics. The intersection is again a four-way stop, with active shops and businesses. The town has a number of well-established old houses to display from the era.

The commemorative tablet refers to the period during which Sherman, with 60,000 troops, camped in Gaylesville, and, reading it, you become amazed that the town could sustain this size force overnight, let alone for days. The tablet was posted outside the small brick building that once served as headquarters, "city" hall, and, later, jail. ((It has a section of wall blown out where a jail break attempt seemed obvious.))

Sherman went back to Atlanta with only part of his troops, leaving most to Gen. Thomas, and proceeded to burn Atlanta.

As with most of the soldiers, they write of the general things around them, and then refer back to the savored events they share with the folks back home. Revery is sweet for soldiers on the battle front.

Kimmel's use of O.V.V.I. referred to the fact that his regiment had become known as the Ohio Veteran Volunteer Infantry, an honor earned by a few groups during the War.

LTR19a

LTR 19b

The next letter is from brother John J. to Ann.

John who has been in Atlanta, in the Ambulance Corps, of the 20 th corps, has been relatively safe.

Letter 20

He writes:

"Atlanta Nov the 1st 1864

Mifs (sic) Ann

Dear Sister:

I recd your vary (sic) welcome letter a few days ago, and was vary (sic) glad to hear from you, especially to hear that you was blefsed (sic) with good health. It is a great blessing to have good health, but far (sic, with "far" underlined by John) greater, to have a pure heart, and a happy Soul. I would like to know how you are getting along in a religious point of view. Do you feel that Sacred love burning upon the altar of your heart, which the world can neither give, nor take away? Do you keep your Soul untarnished and pure? Do you feel that peace within, which none but the christian can feel? Do you feel that joy, which is unexpressible and full of glory? If not, put your trust in God, and pray to him fervantly, day and night, and He will restore you. There is virtue (pg.2)

and power in fervant prayer. I find (to my great joy) when I grow cold and indifferent, if I come to God, acknowledge my sins, and pray fervantly, and earnestly ("for forgiveness", in the space between the upper lines) He always hears and answers my petitions; and causes my Soul to rejoice. There are three things essential to religion, viz: faith, hope, and love. I hope and pray that you may ever be kept faithful.

I have no war news to write. There are no special movements going on here at present. There is but One Corps (the 20th) in Atlanta; The balance of the army is back near the R.R. operating against Hood. It is believed that we (the 20th Corps) will leave here in a few days, and go on a raid; but this is vary (sic) uncertain. The report that Shermans army is in a critical situation, is untrue. We have always had enough to eat, and plenty to do, to keep us out of mischief. There is no danger of starvation here. Forage was a little scarce, but we went out into the country, and got plenty. We will not be permitted to come home this fall to vote.

Please write immediately.
Your affectionate brother
My paper is scarce. (Along border of pg.2) J.J.Huffman"

Atlanta Nov the 7th 1864

Miss Ann:

Dear sister:

I recd, your very welcome
letter a few days ago, and was very glad
to hear from you, especially to hear that
you was blessed with good health. It is a
great blessing to have good health, but
far greater, to have a pure heart, and
a happy soul. I would like to know
how you are getting along in a religious
point of view. Do you feel that sacred
love burning upon the altar of your heart,
which the world can neither give, nor
take away? Do you keep your soul untarnished and pure? Do you feel that peace
within, which none but the christian can
feel? Do you feel that joy, which is unexp-
essible and full of glory? If not, put your
trust in God, and pray to him fervantly, day
and night and he will restore you. There is virtue

LTR20a

and power in fervent prayer. I find (to my great joy) when I grow cold and indifferent, if I come to God, acknowledge my sins, and pray fervently, and earnestly, *for forgiveness*, He always hears and answers my petitions; and causes my soul to rejoice. There are three things essential to religion; viz: faith, hope, and love. I hope and pray, that you may ever be kept faithful.

I have no war news to write. There are no special movements going on, *here* at present. There is but One corps (the 20th) in Atlanta; ~~the balance of the army is back near~~ the R.R. operating against Hood. It is believed that we (the 20 corps) will leave here in a few days, and go on a raid; but this is very uncertain. The report that Sherman's army is in a critical situation, is untrue. We have always had enough to eat, and plenty to do, to keep us out of mischief. There is no danger of starvation here. Forage was a little scarce, but we went out into the country, and got plenty. We will not be permitted to come home this fall to vote.

Please write immediately. Your affectionate brother, A.A.Huffman.

My paper is leave.

LTR20b

NOTES: (Letter 20)

John is again preaching to sister Ann, which he may have felt he was shirking in his last few letters and that he needed to catch-up. The slack nature of the war, for a moment, as he was seeing it, gave him a moment to reflect on where he had left his previous arguments for her benefit.

He gives her a number of tough questions to consider (quietly and to herself) and passes along his strong feelings of how to solve her life problems herself.

He gives Ann the reassurance that Shermans army is NOT in a critical situation as has been reported outside. We can only hope that he was making a "valued judgment" and not just passing along the "party line". As a soldier with the character he demonstrates, he very likely is passing along a true assessment of Sherman's army's condition!

The reference to "foraging" is interesting, because the Union Army depended on this exclusively for their food supplies after they cast themselves loose from their supply bases near Atlanta. The recent harvest had been a good one and the rebels were unable to destroy, remove or hide much at all.

The march through Georgia was shockingly easy for the army and proved Sherman's theory that the Confederacy's defenses were a hollow shell.

Note along the left border of pg.2 says: "My paper is scarce", so he terminated his thoughts abruptly and signed it, without the address he always previously had included.

This is the first admission that they will not be home to vote this fall.

As the war progressed positively for the troops from the north, the news from the homefront worsened as cold weather and sickness set in there, mostly typhoid at this time.

Letter 21

Ann's sister Christine writes to her;

"New Cumberland Ohio
Nov. the 3rd / 64

Miss Ann

Dear sister

Your most welcome letter came to hand this (most) (sic, and crossed off) morning and recd (sic) my careful perusal and we were very glad to hear that you was well but I am sorry to tell you of the very sad scene that has occurred here Peter Hoopingarner died on last sunday (sic) and was buried on Monday (sic) He died with the typhoid fever Elizabeth and marion (sic) laying to bed with it a good while but then they got better Peter took it and he was sick (pg,2)

just three weeks and Rebecca Jane had it to (sic) but she has got better and now Barbara Ann is laying with it but she has just took it and we don't know how bad she will get and the old woman has a very hard time of it for Lizzy and her is not able to do much yet and they can not get any girl for a great many people is afraid to go (sic) and Ann Eliza Suiter is laying very bad with it and the last we heard from her she was still getting worse the doctor has not much hopes of her recovery and Mary Wingate had it very bad to (sic) but she is getting better (pg.3)

it is very sickly here Aunt Polly Huffman has been sick about a month and Mary Ann Mansfield is sick also but it is their old complaints that ails them (all sic) you said you wanted to know if we had heard from the boys lately George's got a letter from John last friday (sic) and he had not been very well for several days but he was better when he rote (sic) he said David was well. we have not heard from W. Bowman since he was taken prisoner Wesley Hoopingarner had deserted the army

Mary talks of coming in this fall but her folks think she had better not until they all get well for it is (Pg.4)

very sickly here and the fever is catching and she might take it. we are all well except Mathilda has the ague they was working at William Welshes below Sandyville close to the water and she took it while she was there I must close my letter and I want you to show it to Mike Kimmels for Hoop(ingarner) has not wrote to tell them about Peter being dead So write at receipt

Your sister
C.J.Huffman
I want you to write immediately"

NOTES: (Letter 21) on CJHuffman to Ann letter, Nov3,1864:

Christine, Ann's sister, writes to report the horrendous state of affairs at home with typhoid being rampant and people all around being sick, dying, and in weakened recovery-state. She notes that not enough neighbors are available to help all those needing help, as well being afraid for their own lives because of the typhoid fever.

Chrissey reports to Ann that their brother John (J.J.Huffman) may not be well although he has written to Ann recently and said he was well. He may be keeping their spirits up by protecting them from some of the facts.

Chrissey is the first to mention that the men's friend, Wesley Hoopingarner, (and mentioned in Letter 2 by William Bowman when they first arrived in camp together in the 126th OVI in Parkersburgh Va), has deserted the US Army.
(Keep tuned to further developments here.)

You begin to see the tie-in from the Huffmans to the Kimmels and to the Hoopingarners as close family friends of the past.

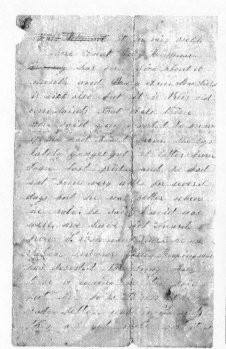
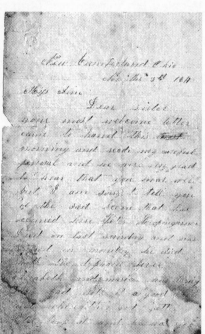

LTR21a

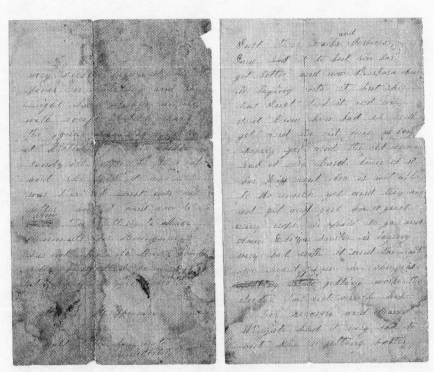

LTR21b

We are short of letters for a period through November and December, 1864, while the war progresses and the sickness continues and recedes, until finally in January, C.J. Huffman again writes Ann with an update:

Letter 22

She writes:

> "New Cumberland O
> Jan the 8th/ 65

Mifs Ann Huffman

Dear Sister

This sabbath morning finds me seated for the purpose of answering your epistle which came to hand a few weeks ago and recd (sic) my careful perusal and we were very glad to hear that you was (sic) well There is a great deal of sickness here this winter Barb Hoop (Hoopingarner) has got well again and the rest of the family are all well except the old man He is still very poorly John Suitors family have had a very hard through (sic) of it they have all had the fever except Dan George and (pg.2) Reebecca (sic),(sic) and Lovina and John died about two weeks ago John was just taking it when Lovina was buried and he was sick just one week but the rest are all getting better Mary Allbaugh (sic) had the fever too but she has got well again and her mother was sick at the same time she has A (sic) young son and Catherine Allbaugh (sic) was working there Finley McCreery has come home again from Indiana He has bought land there there(sic) and he is going back in the spring and John talks of going along Henry Misor had got the wife at last and I have given up all hope of A (sic) man but he got A woman that is a match for him for this is the third man she has had and if (Pg.3)

he stays with her it will be the first one for the other two both left her She has two children Her name is Harriet Binkley Henry has been going to all the balls he could hear of and spend his money every way and his children at home half naked and not much to eat he is as onry (sic, for ornery) as the devil wants him to be and John and Ruham (sp?) goes to the balls and all the onry (sic) company they can find Georges expects an increase in their family if no bad luck That is the reason till (sic, for Mathilda) told you she had not been to meeting for some time for when he comes over here she creeps around like she is afraid It will be about one month but I expect she has told you before this time GW Strawns folks is very much dissatisfied you do not write to them (Pg.4)

we recd a letter from John yesterday and him and David are both well George Strawn is teaching school this winter Uncle David Huffman recd a letter from WM Bowman once more and he is still A (sic) prisoner in South Carolina I have no thing more to write this time So no more at present

C. J. Huffman

P.S. I did not know that New Cumberland was moved I seen you directed your letter to New Cumberland Carroll Co I thought that New Cumberland was in Tucarawas Co You also forgot your capital letters on the back of your letter (all sic)"

NOTES on letter 22, of Jan 8th, 1865:

This is a curious comment from C.J. since she does not always use proper capitals and punctuation herself.

This letter may punctuate the fact that the folks at home did not know where the war locations were. C.J. refers to the prison in South Carolina. Although is not known for sure, the 126th OVI may have been sent from one prison to another in North Carolina, in South Carolina, and Georgia, before arriving at Camp Sumter, Georgia (now Andersonville Prison). At the time of this letter, however, William Bowman had been in Georgia's Camp Sumter for six months, and had arrived there within the first month after he was captured (May 6 to June 2) so he could not have been moved around very much. It is more likely that they did not know that the prison was in Georgia.

C.J. seems resolved that she may not find a man for her life, since this is the first time she mentions it, but other girls around the community have been getting married rather quickly when their boys come home on furlough.

C.J. confides in her younger sister about the fact that their sister-in-law Mathilda is expecting another child. It seems strange that her husband, George, is so upset about it!

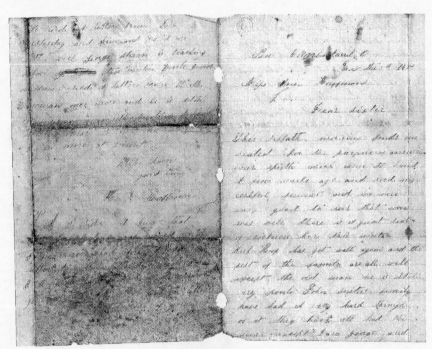

LTR22a

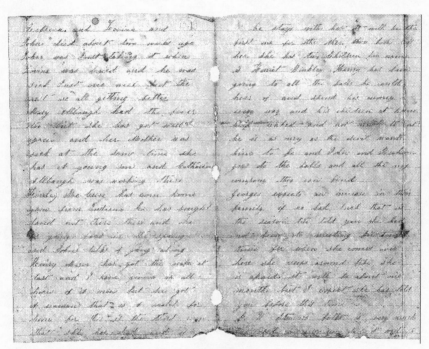

LTR22b

After passage of another two months, Mathilda sends Ann a letter, in March 1865:

Letter 23

She writes:

"New Cumberland O
March the 6th 65

Miss Eveann Huffman

Pretty Sister

how glad I am that I have the strength to write to you in answer to your kind letter which I rec't too (sic) weeks ago and was very glad to hear from you but was sorrow (sic) to hear that you was crippled in your sholder (sic) but I hope that you are well again well Anne I have some gloryous (sic) knews (sic) to tell We have one of the prettyist (sic) babes that ever was born it was two weeks old yesterday (pg.2)

it weighed Seven pounds when it was born Aint it a jolly wormer Kate was here and took care of us agin (sic) George is a making sugar this year He is in the camp and our little girls are a washing and I am a rocking the cradle and writing as the cradle rested six years it goes very well (the cradle) I want you to get a very nice name and send it to me for our babe You wanted me to ask mother wether (sic) you had the mumps and have not seen mother yet but Kate says she thinks you had (pg.3)

you wanted to know if we heard from Bowman lately We heard from him in Nov last and not since I do hope he will be exchanged tell me if you ever hear of Wes Hoop (sic,

Hoopingarner) we got a letter from our dear brother last week they was well there is a great deal of sickness hear (sic) at this time Poor Anne Suiter had to leave this wourld (sic) I hope for a better one she died last monday She took sick in nov. Her little Becky is very low The rest of the family is all better (Pg.4)

there is a great excitement hear (sic) The boys are nearly all volinteering (sic) I will give you some of their names George Strawn Isaac Dilley Isaac Sparks John Misor Sam Wingate James Mills Uncle George Barricks George Luther Tressel They are all gone now God only knows who will go next George has paid twenty five dollars this time to clear our twp (sic, short for "township:) he has paid eighty in all old aunt Polly Huffman is very low Catherine Albaugh is very bad with the fever Now tell us when you are coming home. Write soon good by Your sister

Mathilda Huffman

(written upside down in the upper margin page 4)

Hoops are all well Barb was hear (sic) yesterday She brought me some sweet cakes

(upside down on upper margin pg. 3 and pg 2)

We are all well babe and all I wish you were hear(sic) to get some tafy (sic, "taffy")"

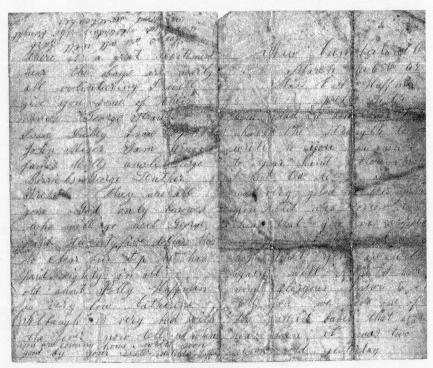

LTR23a

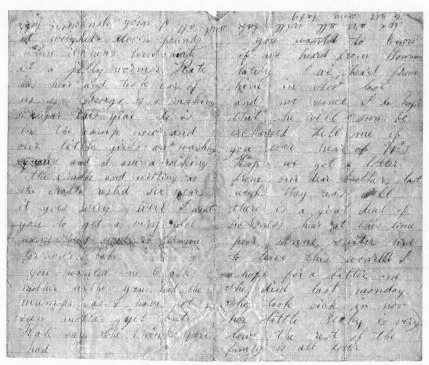

LTR23b

NOTES: (Letter 23)

Very newsy and lists the soldiers drafted, although only months before the end of the war. Barrick listed above is a family member of my great grand mother's mother's family. She married Charles Sherrod (who started Sherrodsville, Ohio,) and produced Lizzie Sherrod, who married Patrick Dougherty, Aunt Becky's father and the patriarch of our US family. The names Barrick and Sherrod both appear as honoring street names in Sherrodsville, Ohio.

SPECIAL NOTE:

Eli Barrick was a member of the 126th OVI and was involved in the Battle of the Wilderness in May 1864. Our William Bowman, along with others of the 126th were captured at the Wilderness by the Confederates and were taken as prisoners from VA, down through South Carolina, and into Georgia, several ending up in Camp Sumter. One of the features of that battle was the fact that the woods were set afire by the intensity of the cannon fire, and many of the disabled-wounded, as well as the bodies of the killed, were burned before they could be recovered. Eli Barrick was one of those whose body was "burned up", but he had been shot dead in the head and did not "suffer" from the fire. (Note comments of our correspondent in Letter 15.)

Mathilda has just had her new baby and asks Ann to find a name for it (an honor for the younger Ann). At two weeks old, the baby does not have a specific identity yet. This may have been "standard" practice then due to the number of babies that died before they got very old in the harsh conditions we are finding the families, now, in this disease-infested winter.

Mathilda notes that their twins girls are six years old since the cradle hasn't been used for that long. She again brags on the fact of her babe being the "prettyist" ever born. (She also had pride in the looks of her twins, as we recall.)

Chrissey sends the next letter to Ann within a couple days to refresh the news. She writes:

Letter 24

"New Cumberland O
March the 9th / 65

Mifs (sic) Ann Huffman

Dear Sister

This evening finds me seated for the purpose of answering your letter which came to hand some time ago and we were very glad to hear that you was well but there is a great deal of sicknefs (sic) here this winter. John Suitors (Suiters?) Family have had it hard through with the typhoid fever and Mrs Suiter and two of the children died with it and Catharine and Raebecca (sic) are (? probably "aren't") died yet but they are getting better They have had the fever in the family about five months (pg.2)

and they have all had it except Dan and George, and Catharine Albaugh had the fever too but she is now getting better. I suppose you have heard the news over at Georges they have a great big young daughter it weighed over eleven pounds at first—I do not know what it would [weigh], ((written below the line)) now something lefs (sic) than a hundred I expect that it is pretty near three weeks old there is a great many boys enlisting and I will give you the name of those that I know James Mills Samuel Wingate Isac (sic) Sparks William Sparks Isac (sic) Dilly (sic) Thomas McKaskey Columbus Cooper George Strawn and William Luther Tressel They have enlisted for one year and they get five hundred dollars township bounty one hundred government bounty and twenty dollars a month while in service (Pg.3)

George Strawn was here last wednesday and he said they were going to start next Monday aunt Polly Huffman is laying sick yet and I do no (sic) think she will ever get any better for she is very weak She has to spit in cloths nearly all the time and they have been sitting up with her nearly all winter and some of us has to go down every few nights I believe I have nothing more to write this time

No more at present
your sister
C J Huffman
write soon

P.S. Said (?, "Sadie") says you must hurry and get married and fetch your man in here and let us see him if you can't read this send it back and I will read (?) it for you fo(sic) I wrote it with a short stick (graphite pencil lead)." (This part is written around the corner up the margin on the pg.3, even though she has an entire page (4.) left if she turned it over.)

New Cumberland O

March the 9th 65

Miss Ann Huffman.

Dear Sister
This evening finds me seated
for the purpose of answering your
letter which came to hand
some time ago and we were very
glad to hear that you was well
but there is a great deal of
sickness here this winter.
John Suiters family have had
it hard through with ~~the~~
the Typhoid fever and Mrs Suiter
and two of the children died
with it and Catharine and Rebecca
are died yet but they are getting
better they have had the fever
in the family about five months

LTR24a

and they have all _____ it
_____ I am and George and
Catharine although _____ _____
_____ _____ _____ is now getting
_____ I suppose you have heard
_____ was at Georges they have
a great big _____ daughter it
weighed eleven pounds at first
I do not know what it would
_____ something less than a hundred
I expect it is pretty near three
weeks old there is a great _____
_____ inlisting and I will give you
the names of those that I know
James Mills Samuel Wingate _____ _____
William Sparks Isaac Dilly Thomas
_____ Columbus Cooper _____
George Stewart and William _____
_____ they have enlisted for _____
year and they _____ get _____ hundred
dollars township bounty one hundred
government bounty and _____ dollars
a month while in service

George Stearns was here last wednesday
and she said they was going to
start next monday Aunt _____ _____
is laying sick yet well I do not think
she will ever get any better for she
is very weak she has to _____ _____
_____ nearly all the time and they
have been sitting up with her
nearly all winter and some of us
has to go down every few nights
I believe I have nothing more to
write this time

no more at present
your sister
C. J. Huffman

Write soon

P. S. David says you must
hurry and get married and
fetch your man in here and
let us see him
if you cant read this send it
back and I will read it for you
_____ I write at _____ _____ _____

NOTES: (Letter 24)

C J seems to be joking about 'reading it for her', although she doesn't usually joke in her letters.

C J seems to report different news than the others Mathilda says her baby was seven pounds when it was born but C J reports it at eleven pounds, a fact Mathilda might not be comfortable with! C J also expresses her dry humor when discussing the baby's weight as being "something lefs than a hundred", since the baby is now 3 weeks old!! A little sarcasm toward her sister-in-law?!

Letter 25

This is a return to the soldiers' letters, and the reality of the War, being from John J Huffman to his sister, Ann, and referring to their brother, David.

John writes:

"Goldsboro North Carolina
March 28 / 65

My Dear Sister;

I know it will be sad news to hear of the death of our Dear Brother David! He was mortally wounded in a charge of the rebel works, on the 16th inst. ("instant", referring to the date) after intense suffering of nearly ten days he departed this life on the 25th about midnight. This will be painful news to you: but I can recomend (sic) Christ as a Comforter. go to him, and He will sustain you. I am sorely afflicted. I feel as though I had lost the dearest, and only friend I had, here in the army, but Christ is my comforter: when I come to Him He sustains me (pg.2)

I ask the assistance of your prayrs (sic) I feel the need of them. you have mine daily. Not being certain that you are in Ind. ("Indiana", sic) yet, I will write nomore (sic) at this time. I would ask you to live so that you may [meet] (written between the lines) our Dear Brother in Heaven. He gave evidence before he died, that he was going to Christ. Please write soon, and give me me (sic) a word of consolation.

Your aggrieved brother,
J. J. Huffman
Ambulance Corps
2nd Brig. 3 Div 20th A.C.
Goldsboro, N. C."

NOTES: (Letter 25)

More evidence of John's dedication to his religion, and his willingness to share it with his family and to help them be comforted by their faith. Note the proper use of capital letters when referring to others, and to the "He" and "Him" when referring to "God" and "Christ". Ever the "teacher" by example, he carries it into words like brother and sister when referring to his family members.

This letter reaches to me through the years. To have felt that the brothers lived and fought together and that this happened within a month of the end of the War, is certainly tragic!

This must have been a tough letter to write since he and David were so close and traveling together throughout the war. John continues with the 20th Corps.

Goldsboro North Carolina

March 28: /65

My Dear Sister:

I know it will be sad news to you to hear of the Death of our Dear Brother David! He was mortally wounded in a charge on the rebel works, on the 16" inst. after intense Suffering of nearly Ten days, he departed this life on the night of the 25" about midnight. This will be painful news to you; but I can recommend Christ as a Comforter go to him, and He will sustain you. I am sorely afflicted. I feel as though I had lost the dearest, and only friend I had, here in the army. but Christ is my comforter; when I come to him He sustains me.

LTR25a

I ask the assistance of your prayers. I feel a need of them. you have mine daily. Not being certain that you are in S.C. yet, I will write nomore this time. I would ask you to live so, that you may meet our Dear Brother in Heaven. He gave evidence before he died, that he was going to Christ. Please write soon, and give me me a word of consolation

Your aggrieved brother,

H.S. Huffman

Ambulance Corps

2" Brig. 3 Div. 20" A.C.

Goldsboro N.C.

LTR25b

Approaching the end of the War, the Confederates found it increasingly difficult to feed their army, as well as the prisons, and to provide them with the minimal supplies necessary for the sustenance of the men, (prisoners and soldiers, both), they began releasing prisoners in exchanges with the north where they could. It was not so much to get their exchanged prisoners back into action on the "right" side, as it was to relieve the overcrowding in the prison camps and to decrease the need of personnel to attend to the camps. In the exchange, the trains and vehicles carrying released troops one direction, were used to transfer the opposing troops being released in the other direction, which point was observed by citizens along these routes.

William Bowman was released from Camp Sumter (today known as "Andersonville Prison") and has made his way home to Ohio, by the time of his next letter, on April 25, 1865.

He gets home and finds that his favored correspondent, Ann Huffman, no longer lives in Tuscarawas County, Ohio, but has moved to Indiana.

He writes her:

Letter 26

"April 25 1865
New Cumberland Tuscarawas Co. Ohio

Miss Ann Huffman

Dear friend

it is with pleasure that I seat my sealf (sic) this morning to let you know that I am well and I hope when these few lines come to hand they will find you enjoying the same great blessing of health I received your kind letter yesterday and I was glad to hear from you once more and to hear that you are enjoying good health I was sorry to hear that David was dead I thought we would get home to gether (sic) and we would have some good times to gether (sic) but I hope John and the rest of the boys will get home, the prospect of the war being over and I hope it will The knabors (sic) is all well as far as I know your aunt mary is not getting anny (sic) better I do not think she will get well at tall (sic) (pg.2)

Ruth J Davy told me to write to you that she is well and hearty and as big a mischief as ever Ann I have a verry (sic) lonsome (sic) time since I come home but I have good times I had hard times all last summer I think I will have better times this summer the boys is all gone from her (sic) but a few I will tell you a little about Wes Hoopingarner he deserted and joined the rebbel (sic) army I never thought he has that little principal (sic) a bout him as that comes to he never need come back in this country when I was in prision (sic) I said that I would die befour (sic) I would gow (sic) out a (sic) take the oath of a leigence (sic) I thought it was more honor to die and

(sic) honerable (sic) death than to gow (sic) ot (sic, for 'out')
and disgrace my sealf (sic)

I have got only four mounths (sic) to serve anny (sic) more
but I do not think there will be anny (sic) more fighting (pg.3)
You must come home when John and the boys comes
home I have not got verry (sic) mutch (sic) to write at the
preasnt (sic) time I will write more the next time you must
excuse all bad writing and spelling sow (sic) is(?, "I") will close
for the preasant (sic) Write as soon as this comes to hand
from your fried (sic) Wm Bowman

Miss Ann Huffman
good by"

NOTES: (Letter 26)

William is missing his buddies from his home town, who by
now have nearly all been taken into the war. He is home from
the prison camp, and on furlough, but realizes that he is still
lonesome without the "boys" being there. He hopes that this
summer will be better than last summer when he recovered in
the prison.

He is very vocal about his displeasure with Wes
Hoopingarner, a friend with whom he went into the first camp
at Parkersburgh Va when they entered the war. Obviously
good friends, who watched each other's backs at one time,
William felt disdain for the friend that he felt had violated
their mutual trust, friendship and patriotism. Strong words,
threatening Wes to "NEVER NEED COME BACK IN THIS
COUNTRY." Easily understood, when William had survived
a long period in what, it could be argued, was among the
worst Prison camps the civilized world has ever seen. William
continues, "WHEN I WAS IN PRISON I SAID THAT I WOULD
DIE BEFORE I WOULD GO OUT AND TAKE THE OATH

OF ALLEGIANCE. I THOUGHT IT WAS MORE HONOR TO DIE AN HONORABLE DEATH THAN TO GO OUT AND DISGRACE MYSELF . . . ."

The more William wrote in this letter he apparently became more and more upset as evidenced by his deteriorating spelling.

William had obviously thought about the rumors he may have heard about being a "turncoat" and getting out of the war. His honor and commitment were NOT about to let him do anything like that!

William's comment to Ann that she should come home (referring to Ohio) when her brother John J Huffman and the boys come home (from the war, referring to the local friends) speaks to his desire to see her in Ohio (quite a bit more convenient than traveling to Indiana, since he obviously likes her a lot.)

April 3th 1865

N. Cumberland Tuscarawas Co.
Ohio

Miss Ann Huffman

Dear friend it is with pleasure
that I seat my self this morning
to let you know that I am
well and I hope when these few
lines come to hand they will
find you enjoying the same great
blessing of health I received your
kind letter yesterday and I was
glad to here from you once more
and to here that you ar enjoying
good health I was sorry to here
that David was dead I thought
we would get home together
and we would have some good
times together but I hope John
and the rest of the boys will
get home the prospect of the war
being over and if not it will the
labourers is all well as far as I
know your aunt mary is not getting
anny better I do not think she will
get well attall

LTR26a

LTR26b

Switching again to the 85th Ind Vol, we hear from J. J. Huffman, who is in Raleigh, N.C.

Letter 27

He writes:

"Raleigh, N.C. April 28th 1865

Dear Sister:

Your kind and affectionate letter of the 16th inst. came to hand yesterday, but I cannot answer all your questions at present. I have not time, I expect to come home and tell them to you: which will be more pleasant than writing. Johnston has surrendered his entire army to Gen Sherman and the war is virtually over—hostilities have ceased and we expect to start for Washington City (Wash, DC) next Monday. I expect to be in Indiana about the first of June. (Pg.2)

and perhaps I will come by and See you, and if you want to come home with me, you can do So. I have not time to write more at present. I will expect a reply by the time I reach Washington. Do not delay writing.

Your affectionate brother

addrefs J. J. Huffman
Co I. 85th Ind. Vol.
2nd Brig. 3rd Div. 20 AC

Mifs (sic) E. A. Huffman"

NOTES: (Letter 27)

It is interesting that fighting in North Carolina seemed to have continued until Johnston surrendered his army. So while the soldiers and civilians further north were celebrating Lee's surrender, hostilities were still going on elsewhere for about two weeks.

John and the 85th Indiana probably made it back to Washington for the Grand Review of May 25 and 26 in which tens of thousands of Union soldiers paraded down Pennsylvania Avenue in a great celebration of their dedication, sacrifice and final victory.

This letter is pretty short, covering only a little more than one and a half of the four pages available for writing, emphasizing the urgency John felt, which caused him to ignore answering his sister's questions.

Raleigh N. C.

April 28'/65

Dear Sister,

Your kind and
affectionate letter of the 16"
inst. came to hand yesterday;
but I cannot answer all
your questions at present,
I have not time, I expect
to come home and tell them
to you; which will be
much more pleasant
than writing. Johnston
has surrendered his entire army
to Gen. Sherman, and the
war is virtually over — hostilities have ceased, and we
expect to start for Washington
City next monday. I
expect to be in Indiana
about the first of June,

LTR27A

and perhaps I will come
by and see you, and if
you want to go home with
me, you can do so.
I have not time to
write any more at present.
I will expect a reply by
the time I reach Washington.
Do not delay writing.
Your affectionate
brother

F. P. Huffman
Address { Co. P 85" Ind. Vol.
2" Brig. 3" Div 20 A.C.

Miss E. A. Huffman

LTR27b

Well, the War is over, by most accounts, and the folks at home are receiving notes and letters from their soldiers as to what to expect and when to expect it. This letter from Mathilda to sister-in-law, Ann, repeats the messages, some of which we have known since April, but the anxiety of the times, and the uncertainties of the plans, and the interminable "delay of the mails" we still experience today (2013), has this letter posted in mid-May.

Letter 28

Mathilda writes:

"New Cumberland O
May the 18th 65

Miss E. A. Huffman

Kind sister

I rec't your letter two weeks ago and I will try and write I would had wrote sooner (all sic) but was waiting for a letter from brother John we rec't a letter from him yesterday he is well and he is coming home well sister glory to God the war is over but sorry to say we have lost a dear brother indeed but Gods (sic) will be done we had to give up our good old president but wo unto the rebbels now(all sic) (pg.2)

poor old uncle George Hoopingarner died last Sunday about three oclock (sic) PM and was buried Monday they met at the house at one O (sic) and the surmond (sic) was preached at the house by McCale it was a large burian (sic) old aunt Polly Huffman is very poorly mothers are all well George works at his trade he gets one dollar and seventy 1.75

(sic) per day and Mary and Maggy goes to school and I and pet ((this is the baby daughter)) are left alone I am making pet a knew (sic) dress she has three to make I got her one and the others was give to her We call her Ruth Christeene

(Mathilda may not have waited for Ann to send a nice name for the new baby, and just went ahead and named her)

She is three months old tomorrow and weighs 20 pounds Lully for the babe (Sing a lullaby for the baby??) I must close and write John a letter Write and tell us when you are coming home Do write soon

Good by Believe yours
Till Huffman (nickname for Mathilda)

PS Nick Hoop wrote home that Wes was taken prisnor (sic) and then inlisted in the rebble army (all sic) and is paroled and will be home soon

Mathilda Huffman

(pg.4)(written very flourishingly)
George Huffman
Mathilda Huffman Mary M Huffman
Maggie Huffman Ruth Huffman
Chew some of my cloves Tell us when your a coming home"

George Huffman
Matilda Huffman
Mary M Huffman
Maggie Huffman
Ruth C Huffman

show some of my
clothes

tell us when your a
coming home

New Cumberland O
May the 18 65
Miss E A Huffman
Kind sister
I recd your letter too welcom
and I will try and
write I would had wrote
soner but was waiting for
a letter from brother
John we got a letter
from mine yesterday he
is well and is coming
home with sister glory
to God the war is over
sorry to say we have lost
dear brother indeed but
Gods will be done
we had to give up our
good old president
but we onto the
rebels now

LTR28a

poor old uncle George
Hoopingarner died last
sunday about three oclock
PM and was buried
monday they met at the
house at one and the
sermond was preached
at the house by mc Call
it was a large barian
old aunty is well and
all the rest of the family
old aunt Polly Huffman
is very poorly brothers
are all well George
works at his trade he
gets one dollar and seventy
five per day and Mary and
Maggy goes to school and
I and pet are left alone
I am making pet a new
dress she has three too
make I got her one

and the others was
give to her we call her
Ruth Christene she is
three months old tomorrow
and weighs 20 pounds
lusty for the babe
I must close and write
John a letter
write and tell us
where you are coming
home do write soon
good by believe your
till Huffman

P S Nick Hoop wrote
home that Wes was
taken prisnor and then
enlisted in the rebble army
and is paroled and will
be home soon
Matilda Huffman

LTR28b

NOTES: (Letter 28)

Mathilda shares her thoughts with the world!

"GLORY TO GOD THE WAR IS OVER.
SORRY TO SAY THAT WE HAVE LOST A DEAR BROTHER, INDEED, BUT GOD'S WILL BE DONE.
WE HAD TO GIVE UP OUR GOOD OLD PRESIDENT, BUT WO UNTO THE REBBELS NOW!"

We'll never know whether the seven (or was it eleven?) pound baby was really 20 pounds at 3 months, or whether it WAS closer to 100 pounds, as Chrissey had surmised.

Wes Hoopingarner was paroled by the Confederates, but it is not clear yet whether he ever came back to New Cumberland, Ohio. He had received poor acceptance by his former friends when he turned-coat, while they defended their country.

A further letter from John J. Huffman was sent from Indianapolis, Indiana, to his sister, Ann, with more details of his plans as he becomes discharged from the 85th Indiana Volunteer Infantry.

He writes:

Letter 29

"Indianapolis, Ind
June 28 / 65

Dear Sister

I am now in Indianapolis, Ind and expect to be paid off [today] (written between lines) and receive my final discharge. I will then return to Clay Co. Ind. where I expect to remain for two or three weeks, and then I think I will go to Ohio, and if you wish to go with me, I will be very happy to stop in Henry Co. and have you go home with me. I expect to be ready to Start in a little more than three weeks. (Pg.2)

You will please write immediately on the receipt of this, and let me know what you will do. My health is good and I hope you enjoy the same blefsing (sic).

Yours affectionately
J. J. Huffman

direct to Bowling Green
Clay Co. Ind."

INDIANA SOLDIERS
The Pride of the State

THIS SHEET OF PAPER AND ENVELOPE IS FURNISHED
BY THE
INDIANA SANITARY COMMISSION.
Being purchased with Funds contributed by the
SOLDIERS' FRIENDS AT HOME.

Fly little missive to my cherished home,
And cheer the loving hearts so sad so dear;
I'll follow when to Illinois I am come,
And leave "OUR FLAG" to restore floating here!
T A— Robins.

Indianapolis Ind.
June 28" /65

Dear Sister:

I am now in Indianapolis Ind, and I expect to be paid off to day and receive my final discharge. I will then return to Cloz Co Ind, where I expect to remain for two or three weeks, and then I think I will go to Ohio, And if you wish to go with me, I will be very happy to stop in Henry Co. and have you go home with me. I expect to be ready to start in a little less than three weeks.

LTR29a

You will please write immediately, on the receipt of
this, and let me know
what you will do.
My health is good
and I hope you enjoy
the same blessing
Yours affectionately
P. P. Huffman

Direct to Bowling Green
Clay Co. Ind.

LTR29b

NOTES: (Letter 29) on JOHN J. HUFFMAN: (85 th Indiana Volunteer Infantry)

It is known that John was in Indianapolis for discharge and was paid off on June 28, 1865.

His discharge papers show him as being mustered out that date, by the 85th Ind Vol Inf.

It is ironic and tragic that he was probably way-laid there and HAS NEVER RETURNED. Family efforts to recover his body (or any other information) have been futile. Suffice it to say that John J. Huffman was probably ATTACKED and KILLED by robbers who preyed on soldiers after they received their final pay-off, and was KILLED after the end of the Civil War. Considering all his extensive family plans revealed in his letters, it is not likely he took the money and 'ran'. He was never seen again, and more recent investigation through computer resources available in 2013 have revealed no connections. His family lost two super-quality men, patriotic and God-fearing, and the community lost potential leaders, as well.

Ann's expectation that John was coming by, to accompany her back to Ohio, was disrupted by his disappearance and the FINAL TRAGEDY in her Civil War experiences.

NOTES on DAVID HUFFMAN; (85 th Indiana Volunteer Infantry)

John and Ann's brother, David, was wounded in Goldsboro, N.C. serving with the 85th Ind. Vol. Inf, on the 16 th of March, 1865 and died of his wounds on the 25 th of March, 65, within three months of the end of the War, having made it nearly all the way through with his brother John.

NOTES on JOSEPH. W. KIMMEL: (51 st Ohio "Veteran" Volunteer Infantry)

After the War he returned home and, although he regarded Ann Huffman a special friend, he married Matilda June Moser, a local girl, in 1878. He had been born on June 6, 1846.

He went to Wittenburg College and Hanuma Seminary, graduating in 1875, and became a Lutheran Minister and Missionary. He was ordained by the Pennsylvania Synod at Gettysburg, Pa. In his career, he organized 18 churches under the General Synod.

He retired as a Lutheran Minister and died on August 15, 1906, in Lincoln, Nebraska, and rests in Wyuka (sic) Cemetery there.

The Kimmel family had a prominent presence in the Rose Township of Carroll County, Ohio, for a long time before Joseph came along, with his Dad having donated the land for building a United Brethern Church there, and, later, the land for a country school. Both were considered "firsts" in that area.

He entered some of his recollections of the Civil War into the Ohio Historical Society in the early 1900's as events he related to his daughter. (Available on Internet.)

The letters we have from Joseph Kimmel, and the references we have to him and his family during the war and shortly after, are not likely in his collection of memoirs since they were received directly by our Ann Huffman. There is not an obvious way these letters could have been duplicated by him at that time for later use. We will addend his collection in good time to those same resource locations.

NOTES on GEORGE HILLICKS:—"FLAGSTAFF"
(Cpl, Co. L, 16 th Illinois Volunteer Cavalry)

George entered the service at Urbana, Illinois, on March 5, 1863, for a 3 year term (mustered in on April 16, 1863, at Camp Butler, IL.)

He was captured at Jonesville Va., date unknown, which was located about 49 miles N.W. of Johnson City, TN, or about 117 miles S.E. of Lexington, Ky.

He was listed as a corporal while he served as a Prisoner in Camp Sumter (Andersonville).

He became famous as the fellow known as "Flagstaff" due to his extreme height after he kept growing throughout his time in prison to become the tallest inmate in Camp Sumter. He was memorialized in the artist's sketch, and, later, in the book, "This was Andersonville", by John McElroy.

He was mustered out on August 19, 1865 at Nashville, TN.

NOTES on WILLIAM BOWMAN: (Private, 126 th Ohio
Volunteer Infantry)

William was mustered out at Camp Chase, near Columbus, Ohio, on the 23 rd of June, 1865, as a private in Company G of the 126 th Regiment of the Ohio Volunteer Infantry, having served most of the three years since his enlistment on August 4 th, 1862.

He received $257.99 extra pay (3 months extra) beyond his due settlement on Jun 6th, 1866. He had spent from May 6 th, 1864, as a Confederate Prisoner of War until we have evidence of his exchange in April, 1865.

His letter from home, in New Cumberland, Ohio, on April 25, 1865, expresses his thankfulness of being home, but his lonesomeness, since most of his friends have been drafted, or killed. He hopefully looks forward again to the good times with everyone, when many of them, too, return, and thinks he "will have better times this summer".

He notes the "prospect of the war being over, and I hope it will".

This letter, (No. 26) was written Apr 25, although the record shows his discharge happened on April 23, he just hadn't known yet. He entered the service as a farmer, and after receiving his discharge at Camp Chase, near Columbus, returned to the farm, back in Tuscarawas County, Ohio.

Although he was a Private during the war, he joined the Grand Army of the Republic (GAR) and rose to the rank of Colonel of J.I. Alexander post, No. 474, by July of 1896. As were many others, he was a dedicated soldier for his entire life

NOTES on WILLIAM BOWMAN and ANN HUFFMAN:

They apparently wasted no time in refreshing their relationship at the end of the War, and they were married on September 10, 1867.

Having come from a hearty, long-living family, William and Ann produced three children, two daughters and my Grand Uncle, Jesse Clyde Bowman. Jesse, born June 6, 1873, died on Feb. 23, 1975 at the age of 101 years and 8 ½ months.

William was born in 1845 and died in Tuscarawas County, Ohio, in 1925.

Ann was born in 1841 and died in 1920.

Both are buried, together, in New Cumberland, Tuscarawas County, Ohio, in the Methodist Church cemetery.

As was obvious by this time, the War is certainly over. Having grieved over their lost relatives and friends, life is attempting to return to normal for the women back home, their families and the returned troops.

Mary Kimmel, sister of Joseph W., has been at home throughout the War, and, while not very well-educated, she has been busy keeping up with the family, friends and neighbors, while trying to tend to her immediate family's needs and their desire to move into a new place. Although it is somewhat difficult to read, the following letter demonstrates what the normal "woman back home" went through keeping themselves busy while the War took place.

Letter 30

Letter to Ann Huffman from Mary Kimmel.

August the 16 AD 1865

well ann i take my pen in hand this rainy monday morning to right (sic) to you in answer of your kind letter wich (sic) we received from you last tuesday evening and we was truley (sic) glad to heare (sic) from you and that you reached your home safe and have the pleasure of seeing and finding your friends all weell (sic) i can tell you that we are all well and have been since you left and i hope this will find you all in the great blesing (sic) of health well ann i have been very lonesome since you left the children talkes (sic) of you every day they say you will com (sic) back agin (sic) that evening we came home that you went away that was the drearyest (sic) evning (sic) i saw sence (sic) we liven (sic) at this pace (sic) mike went to praryer (sic) meeting it was too late i did not go i went to milk when i came back from milking before i came nere (sic) the house i herd (sic) the childern (sic) all cry and I hored (sic, for hurried) to the house and asked what they ware (sic) crying for and they said that ann was gon (sic) and wod (sic) come back no more and i could harley (sic) get margret peeseyed fied (all sic, for "pacified") till i tolded (sic) them that you will come back agin so they think you will come back agin and i hope that you will too Mrs root went to prayer meeting that nite and she told me that nany cryed (sic) so she did not now (sic) what to do with her and she asked her what she was crying for and she said whey (sic, for "when") she thinks of ann she could not help crying sow (sic) you may

(Pg. 2) now (sic) the childern (sic) will get home sick to see you if you don't come back annn (sic) is so prety (sic) and sweat (sic, for "sweet) as ever we was at the croos rodes (sic, for "cross roads") meeting yesterday david moer and elen went along ann clark lysia and mary jane grves went along too there was a lare (sic, "large") congreation (sic) there lanchester preached his fairwell (sic) sermon there and it was worth going to here (sic) for i never herd (sic) a better sermon and we went to George yonges (sic, "Youngen's") for dinner there at saferdes and we got a good dinner you now (sic) it is a nomber (sic) one place you now (sic) we was there last fall saferdes folks inquierd (sic, "inquired") about you i must tell you a little about the solgers super (sic, "soldiers supper") that was the next Thursday after you left Mrs gusten and claria and i went together mike was holing (sic, "hauling") wheat he did not go i took anney and margret with me the boys stayed with there (sic) pa i can tell you ther (sic) wore (sic) a great many people there and the beautifullist table that i ever seen

i wish you wold (sic) of been there we had a good time there ann clarke has been here and spent a

day with me sence (sic) you left she said she wod (sic) come and help me cook when we thrash

i expect you want to now (sic) about the health of the neighbors well there has been some sickness sence (sic) you left grammother commones and mille (sic, Milly) and mary ann commones has had the fever but they are about well agin (sic)

(Pg. 3) dan kimmel was sick a few dayes (sic, days) the doctor said he had the biles fever (sic, bilious fever, ((severe vomiting until product is only bile, the stomach is essentially empty, and it produces a fever))) but he is about well agin(sic) i think it is a very lite kind of fever they get over it so soon margret bristle had the fever too i think she had it wore (sic, worse) than eny (sic, any) of them you now (sic) she was sick that day we was there and her childern (sic) wore (sic) all sick at the same time but the childern (sic) has all got well agin (sic) and margret has got rite (sic) smart agin (sic) she and her childern (sic) went along with us yesterday to her mothers and stayed till we come back Mrs root went to her mothers saturday she is coming home today on the train her mother is going to start to virginia to morrow and you now (sic) she had to go and see her before she goes away for fear she will never get to see her eny (any) more she don't like for her mother to go for fera (fear a) smthing (all sic) mite (sic) hapen (sic) ((to)) her one (sic, "on") the rode (sic, road) that she wold (sic) get back no more then you now (sic) mrs root wold (sic) go up she said when she herd (sic) her mother was going she did not sleep eny (sic) the first nite and you now (sic) eny thing (sic) must bee (sic) very bad if she cant sleep june elson is sick she has some soers (sic, sores) on her the doctor said she had a carabonkle (sic, carbuncle) on her back the people all makes fun of it you now (sic) that for the woman she is she has rented her place to a man the name of nolan and I am glad

(Pg.4) of it for I ges (sic, guess) it is the man that will suit her i ges (sic, guess) we will get old jaky summers is (sic, summers') farm and that a good farm and a good house and a good oched (sic, orchard) and plenty of good apples on it he wanted us to moove (sic, move) one (sic, on) it right away so we can make use of the apples his soninlaw is going away next week if we take the place we will seed on it next fall i don't now (sic) yet wat (sic, what) we will do about going there it is a ronge (sic, wrong) time of yere (sic, year) to move will tell you the next letter i rite to you wat we will do i have rote all the importance that i now (sic) at this time i want you to rite and tell me how much it coast (sic, cost) you to go home and when John is going to start from there and how soon you expect to come back and if you herd (sic) enything (sic) of Wes and tell neks (sic, Nick's, (Nick Hoopingarners)) to rite to us tell dan and said (sic, Sadie) that i wish them much luck with thear (sic, their) boy and think if they claime (sic, claim) to bee (sic) eny (sic, any) relation to us that they wod (sic, would) rite once to us talk to you mother and my mother for me for i wold (sic) like to see them ann clark said you should rite to her or the (sic, they) wod(sic) bee insulted Commones girls said you should rite to them or the (sic, they) wod (sic) bee (sic) mad i will get mary ann finkes address (sic, address) and send it in the next letter to you rite to me soon and tell me all the news and secred (sic, secrets) that you now (sic) so no more but remain your kind friend to dath (sic, death)

Mary Kimmel to ann huffman

give my love to all ho (sic, who) in quire of me fair well (farewell)"

upside down on top of Pg.4; "ann I did not now (know) yesterday serten (sic, "certain") if we

wod (sic, would) move but i now (know) today we will we will move as soon as we get our thrashing don (done)"

upside down on top of Pg.3; "i want you to rigt (write) soon and tell me wat (what) you are doing and if you are going to come out this fall you now (know) our barging (bargain) about the carpet and i am wating (waiting) on it"

NOTES: (Letter 30)

While this letter is long and rambling and difficult to read and understand, it shows the depth of other happenings in the lives of the families at home. Many aspects of their lives were not disrupted, and life was pretty much an ongoing event, aside from their men-folk not being there. The women kept the day-to-day events flowing with varying amounts of success, and along with a great amount of community cooperation and assistance, kept the ends together.

Mary Kimmel is not short on words, only the ability to spell them properly, and she does her best to convey the story despite her limited education. She is a font of information, and plans, and expects her addressees to carry out the tasks she lays upon them, such as writing when she says, "Write." She relates the stories of the neighbors and the sick, and includes a reference to her friend with different living "habits", who is renting out her place. Mary even wishes her good luck with the new man. Her letter is quite well-structured with most of the formalities expected of letters of that period, and gracious to all to whom she refers. Spelling and punctuation aside, she has learned the art of letter-writing quite well.

It may be strange that she does not refer to her brother Joseph W., whose letters we included in this piece, since he should be arriving home about this time, from his duty with the 51 st OVVI. We know that he returned, went to school and seminary, married, and became a very successful pastor and missionary.

August the 14th 1865

well ann i take my pen in hand
this rainy monday morning to right to you
in answer of your kind letter wich we
received from you last tuesday evening and
we were truely glad to heare from you
and that reached your home safe and
have the pleasure of seeing and finding
your friends all well & can tell you
that we are all well and have been
since you left and i hope this will find
you all in the great blessing of health
well ann i have been very lonesome
since you left the childern talkes of
you every day they say you will com
back again that morning we come home
that ...

LTR30a

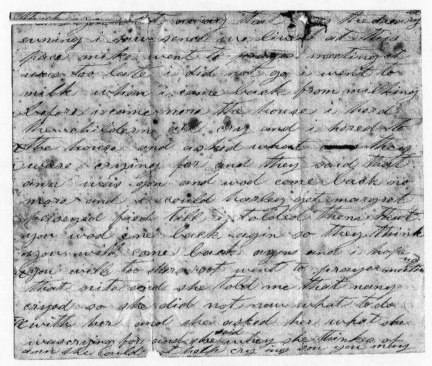

LTR30b

now the childern will get home sick
to see you if you dont come back minney
is as prety and sweat as ever we was at
the cross roads meeting yesterday david moll
and elen went along ann clark lydia
and mary Jane orves went along to
there was a lare congregation there
lonchester preached his fairwell sermon
there and it was worth the going to here for
i never hurd a better sermon and we
went to George yonges for dinner ther
on saperday and we got a good dinner you
now it is a nomber one place you now
we was there last fall saperdy folks
inquired about you i must tell you a
little about the solgers you that
the next thursday after you left Mary
pusten and clarva moll i went
together mike was holing wheat he did
not go i took anney and noregret with
me the boyes stayed with there pap
i can tell you ther ware a great many
people there and the beautifullist
table that i ever seen i wish you
could of been there we had a good time
there ann clarke has been here and
spent a day with me sence you left
she said she wil come and help me
cook when we thresh i expect you want
to now about the health of the neighbacrs
well there has been some sickness sence
you left granmother commones and mille
and mary ann commons has had the
fever but they are about well agin

dan kimmel was sick a few days
the doctor said he had the biles fever
but he is about well again i think
it is a very bad kind of fever they get over
it so soon margret liotte had the
fever too i think she was wore then
eny of them you now she was sick
that day we was there and her
childern ware all sick at the
same time but the childern how
all got well agin and margret has
got rite smart agin she and her
childern want along with us yester
to her mothers and stayed till we come
back she dont want to her mothers
to
on the train her mother is going to
start to vergenia to maorrow and you
now she had to go and see her before
she goes away for fear she will never
get to see her eny more she dont like
to her mother to go for fear anything mite
hapen her one the rode that she wool
get back no more then you now she
dont wool go up she said when
she herd her mother was going she
did not sleep eny the first nite and
you now eny thing mite be very
bad if she cant sleep Jane olson is
sick she has some sores on her the doctor said
it was a caralonele on her back the peope
all makes fun of it you now that for
woman she is she has rented her plase
to a man the name of nolen and i am glad

of it for i eyes it is the man that
will suit her i eyes me will get old
saky sumers is form and that a good
farm and a good house and a good
orchard and plenty of good apples on it
he wants us to moove one it right
away so we can make use of the
appels his soninlaw is going away next
week if we take the place mike will
seed on it this fall i donte now yet
wat we will about going there it is
a ronge tence of yere to move i will
tell you the next letter i rite to you
wat we will do i have wrote you all
the importance that i now at this time i
want you _____ _____ how much
it coast you to go home and when
John is going to start from there and how
soon you expect to come back and if you
herd anything of me and tell nehg to rite
to us tell dan and said that i wish them
much luck with there boy and think
if they clame to bee any relation to us tha
they wod rite once to us talk to you mother
and my mother for me i wod like to
see them own clark again you should rite
to her or he wod bee insulted com moms
is a girls said you should rite to them
or the wod bee ___ i will get mary
ann pinkes adress and send it in the nex
letter to you rite to me soon and tell
me all the news and good speed that you now
is no more but remain your kind friend Ti
dath Moore kimmel to your husmom give my
love to all us in fure but me fair well

LTR30e

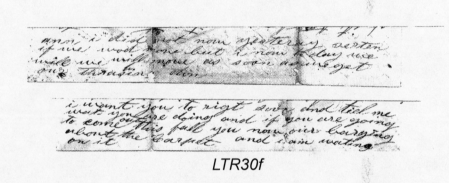

ann i did not now yesterday verten
if we wod move but i now today we
will we will move as soon as we get
our thrasin don

i want you to rigt son and tiel me
wat you are doing and if you are going
to come this fall you now our bargin
about the carpet and i am waiting
on it

LTR30f

Epilogue

Now, having seen the letters, "met" the writers, and "experienced" these stories from their lives, we can better understand how important "Family" was to them.

We have experienced the ravages of their diseases, sickness and, even death. We have shared in their troubles, and their joys, and learned how their faith served them.

We witnessed what wives and families went through to maintain their homes and farms, despite severe winters, and sickness.
We can now appreciate the support offered-, and gratefully received-, among friends and neighbors.

We can also understand their passion for letter-writing, to exercise the new-found freedom it gave them, and to broaden their interactions.

We have seen how much the troops depended on words from "Home", for relieving their anxieties between the War-front needs and the Home-fronts' needs, and the welfare of their loved ones

We have read first-hand reports on several battles and the condition of the Army and troops in the field.

We learned the conditions of the landscapes and cities, after battles, from these reports.

We viewed the conditions of life in a prison camp.

We saw some come home, and some who didn't.

We saw love blossom, and flourish.

We experienced many of the events that filled their daily lives.

We learned about new areas of the country.

We relate to the differences between the 1860's and 2013, especially in the technology area, but recognize that the family and its relationships are not very different in the areas of love, respect, stability, and needs.

We especially recognize the unity and patriotism, we all aspire to-, that were clear in these letters.

We thank the Troops and bless the Patriots.

Tribute to the Honor of Ordinary Citizens

Even now, we again Honor the Ordinary Citizens who stepped up and came forward to defend our young country and to preserve their Freedoms.

We also honor their Families who suffered through diseases and distressing times at home to allow these Patriots to succeed.

We honor those, as well, who recorded these snippets of casual information and who saved their meager communications for posterity.

Without them, we could not have peered through this **Window Upon Our History.**

51 St Regiment Ohio Veteran Volunteer Infantry

Record of Service (3 years)

Organized in September and October, 1861 at Camp Meigs, near Canal Dover, Tuscarawas County, Ohio

Moved to Wellsville, November 3, and then to Louisville, Ky, to Dec. 10, 1861.

To Nashville, Feb 1862, its occupation

15th Brigade, 4th Division, Army of the Ohio, to March, 1862

Nashville to June 1862 (Tullahoma, Pursuit of Bragg) 1863 Murphreesboro, Stone's River, Chickamauga, Lookout Mountain, Seige of Chattanooga, Mission Ridge, Ringgold Gap,

10th Brigade, 4th Diviision, Army of the Ohio, to July, 1862

23rd Independent Brigade, Army of the Ohio, to Aug, 1862

23rd Brigade, 5th Division, Army of the Ohio, to Sept, 1862

23rd Brigade, 5th Division, 2nd Army Corps, to November, 1862

3rd Brigade, 3rd Division, 14th Army Corps, Army of the Cumberland, to Jan. 1863

3rd Brigade, 3rd Division, 21st Army Corps, Army of the Cumberland, to Oct, 1863

In Blue Springs TN, until May, 1864

In May 1864, joined Sherman's Atlanta Campaign

Rocky Face, Resaca, Kingston, Cassville, Dallas, New Hope Church, Allatoona Hills, Marietta, Kennesaw, Chattahoochee River, Peachtree Creek, Siege of Atlanta, Jonesboro, Operations against Hood in North Georgia and Alabama, Nashville Campaign, Duck River, Franklin,

Huntsville (Ala)
To New Orleans, June 16, 1865, and then
To Texas, (Indianola, Green Lake, and Victoria)
2nd Brigade, 1st Division, 4th Army Corps, to Aug, 65
1st Division, 4th Army Corps, to August 1865
Assigned to Dept. Of Texas to October 1865

Final muster out in November, 1865

85 Th Regiment Indiana Volunteer Infantry

Record of Service (3 years)

Organized at Terra Haute, Indiana,—Sept. 2, 1862

Attached to Army of Kentucky—to June 1863

Attached to Army of the Cumberland—Reserve Corps, to October 1863

Attached to Army of the Cumberland—2 nd Brigade, 3 rd Div, 20 th Army Corps, to June, 1865

Louisville, Ky,—to Nashville, TN,—Franklin, TN,

Nashville, TN, June, 12, 1863—Franklin and Murphreesboro, TN, till April, 1864

March to Lookout Valley, TN April 20-28, 1864

Atlanta Campaign

Rocky Face Ridge—May 8-11, Resaca May 14-15, Cassville May 19, Dallas May 22-25, New Hope Church May 25, 1864

Marietta, GA and Kennesaw Mountain, GA June 10-July 2

Lost Mountain, June 15-17, 1864, Golgotha Church, Muddy Creek, Noyes Creek, Kolb's Farm—June 22

Assault on Kennesaw—June 27, Smyrna Campgr'nd—July 4, Chattahoochee River—July 5-17, Peachtree Creek—July 19-20,

Siege of Atlanta—July 22-August 25, 1864

Chattahoochee Bridge—Aug 26-Sept 2

Occupation of Atlanta—Sept 2-November 15, 1864

March to the Sea—November 15-December 10

Seige of Savannah—December 10-21, 1864

Campaign of the Carolinas—Jan to April, 1865

Lawtonville,S.C., Feb 2,—Battle of Bentonville,N.C., March 19-21,

Occupation of Goldsboro, N.C., March 24

Advance on, and Occupation of-, Raleigh, N.C. April 10-14, 1865

<u>Surrender</u> of Johnston and his army.
<u>March to Washington, D.C.</u> via Richmond,VA, April 29-May 19
<u>Grand Review</u>—May 24
Mustered out—June 12, 1865

126 Th Regiment Ohio Volunteer Infantry

Record of Service (3 years)

Organized in Steubenville, Ohio—from Sept. 4, to Oct. 11, 1862
  Mustered out June 25, 1865

Listing of Battles

Martinsburg, W. VA.	June 14, 1863
Wapping Heights, VA.	July 23, 1863
Culpepper C.H., VA.	October 11, 1863
Bristow Station, VA.	October 14, 1863
Bealton and Rappahannock Brdg, VA	October 24 63
Kelley's Ford, VA.	November 7, 63
Locust Grove, VA.	November 27, 1863
Mine Run, VA.	November 26-28, 63
Wilderness, VA.	May 5-7, 1864
Alsop's Farm, VA.	May 8, 1864
Spottsylvania, VA.	May 8-18, 1864
North Anna River, VA.	May 23, 1864
Tolopotomy Creek, VA.	May 30-31,1864
Cold Harbor, VA.	June 1-12, 1864
Bermuda Hundred, VA.	June 18, 1864
Weldon Railroad, VA.	June 22-23, 1864
Monocacy, MD	July 9, 1864
Snicker's Ferry, VA.	July 18, 1864
Charlestown, W.VA.	August 21, 1864
Smithfield, VA.	August 29, 1864
Opequan, VA.	September 19, 1864
Flint Hill, VA.	September 21, 1864
Fisher's Hill, VA.	September 22, 1864
Cedar Creek, VA.	October 19, 1864
Petersburg, VA.	March 25, 1865
Petersburg, VA.	April 2, 1865

Notable Quotations from Ann's Letters

Letter

A   "I have not been so badly beaten since that night and I hope you have not, but it was alright in the morning . . ." Maggie Harper

1   "There is a good deal of bad conduct here, but Wes and I do not take any part in it and I thank god for it that he will protect us from any harm . . ."
". . . man poisand . . . on whiskey , . . . but . . . I do not drink of the filthy stuff . . ."
"we are about 300 miles from home. We came about 500 miles to get here" Wm Bowman, 9/62

2   "We can have about 10,000 of men here in five hours. We have only 2000 here now . . . ."
"The president procolamation says that the war will be over in three months . . . The war cannot last longer than spring . . . ." Bowman 9/62
"There is a great deal of wikedness in camp . . . hard place to do right."

3   ". . . Good many sick . . . hope to god I will keep my health . . . send me some money . . . we have not anny money here . . . . get my boots half-soled." Wm Bowman 1/63

4   from hospital: "<u>There are more soldiers dies of disease than are killed on the battlefield</u>.

has over 300 soldiers died in this place . . . . things appear to be lamentable, but we should be satisfied with our lot. Let it be where it may."

"We have no right to complain, because every complaint we make is against our Supreme Ruler." . . . "asking you to write immediately. I don't ask it because it is fashionable, but because I want you to write." John J. Huffman 2/63

5   during Chickamauga battle John J. Huffman 9/20/63
". . . you say if I get sick, and want any person to wait on me, just let you know and you will be on horses . . . in reply, that you can no more come here than you <u>can go to heaven</u> in a hand basket.
. . . Bragg, fleeing before Rosecrans got
. . . reinforced by Johnson and Lee both
. . . and <u>one of the awfulest battles is being fought, that ever was known in an open field fight</u> . . ."

6   Fosterville, Tn David Huffman 11/20/63
"We have homes built with chimneys to them and are living at the top of the pot . . . no danger of us starving . . . . as long as there is anything in Tennessee, the soldiers will live well."

7   Hardin county, Ohio Catharine McCreery 3/14/64
". . . lots of girls out here and they are just more than a getting married . . .
. . . dyptheria . . . lung fever . . . small pocks"

8   Camp Blue Springs, TN JW Kimmel early 64
". . . still quiet here . . . we have good water . . . times are pretty good and we have plenty to eat."

9   Camp Blue Springs, TN April '64
". . . everyone or to (ought to) marry when they please and who they please" J.W Kimmel

10 ". . . Indiana is not as civilized as you have been accustomed to in Ohio . . .
. . . Indian raids with fair frequency . . . (she young, husband older with children) . . .
. . . If he should pass earlier (than 60 yrs old) you might find yourself with the responsibility of a farm to maintain, and <u>of children, who are not even of your own issue</u> . . ."
"<u>. . . if your mind follow your heart, you have my permission . . .</u>" J.J.Huffman

11 Tullahoma, TN J.J.Huffman 4/25/64
". . . my advice to not go to Indiana need not discourage you as you are already there . . ."
". . . you will find that if you take a friend with you, you will always have friends"

12 Kingston GA during Atlanta Campaign J.J.Huffman 5/64
". . . have not been out from under the sound of cannon for the last two weeks"
". . . Twentieth Corps—commanded by Gen Hooker"

"This country looks very desolate; more than half of the dwellings being evacuated . . . Cassville GA,
. . . our soldiers feasted sumptuously on suppers prepared for the rebs."

13 Camp Sumter, (Andersonville Prison) Wm. Bowman 6/2/64
"<u>. . . I am a prisioner . . . . they have used us middlin' well since we have been prisioners . . .</u>"
Notes on Andersonville Prison . . . Inoculations were first tried to stem diseases

14 ". . . referring to Wilderness Battle . . ." RuthDavey 6/6/64
". . . we had agreat many brave soldiers that fell in that battle They said<u> it was the hards (sic) battle that has bin.</u>"

15 New Cumberland Ohio Mathilda Huffman 7/14/64
(Wilderness Battle) ". . . poor Eli Barrick was <u>shot in the head and his body burnt up . . . OH, MY</u>" . . . . Wesley

Hoopingarner was captured . . . Scarlet rash (scarlet fever) . . ."

17 Atlanta JJ Huffman 9/11/64
"... ATLANTA has fallen . . .
". . . Sherman's brilliant flank moves . . .
". . . entirely destroyed Hood's communications
". . . Sherman cut his army in two . . .
". . . all citizens have to leave the city . . .
". . . this rebellion will play out less than twelve months . . ."

18 (special draft) ". . . there was fifty two drafted out of Rose (township)." 9/28/64 Mathilda Huffman

19 Atlanta, Nov 1, 64 J J Huffman
". . . the report that Sherman's army is in a critical situation, is untrue . . ."
". . . Forage was a little scarce, but we went out into the country, and got plenty . . ."

20 Gailsville, Alabama (Gaylesville) Oct 26, 64 JW Kimmel shortly before Sherman's March to the Sea
". . . have been after the Johnnies again for the last 3 weeks and have stopped to rest for a few days . . . out on picket about 8 miles . . . at bridge . . . pretty good times . . . plenty to eat and drink . . . ."

21 Nov 5, 64 CJ Huffman
". . . very sickly here . . ."
". . . have not heard from W. Bowman since he was taken prisoner . . ."
". . . Wes Hoopingarner had deserted the army."

22 "Great deal of sickness here this winter." CJ Huffman Jan.8, 1865

23 "baby born . . . Wm in prison in SC" (confused as to prison location) Mar. 6, 65 Mathilda Huffman

24 Special Note: Eli Barrick Mar. 9, 65 CJ Huffman
"Great deal of sickness here . . . typhoid fever . . . fever in family for 5 months"
"(baby) something less than 100 pounds I expect . . . pretty near 3 weeks old . . ."

25 Goldsboro, NC Mar.28, 65 J J Huffman
". . . death of our dear brother David . . . wounded on the 16th (died 25th) . . ."
"Report—releases of prisoners in exchanges (to relieve crowding . . .)"

26 New Cumberland, Ohio Apr. 25, 65 Wm Bowman
". . . Wes Hoopingarner . . . deserted and joined rebbel army . . .
". . . he has that little principle about him as that comes to . . ."
". . . he never need come back in this country."
". . . I would die befour I would go out and take the oath of allegiance"
". . . it was more honor to die an honorable death than to go out and disgrace myself . . ."

28 New Cumberland, Ohio May 8, 65 Mathilda Huffman
". . . Well sister, glory to God the war is over, but sorry to say we have lost a dear brother, indeed, but God's will be done! We had to give up our good old president, but WO UNTO THE REBBELS NOW."
"Wes Hoop is paroled and will be home soon"

29 Indianapolis, Ind June 28.'65 J.J. Huffman
". . . expect to be paid off [today] and receive my final discharge . . ."
". . . (intends to stop by Henry County to take sister Ann to Ohio with him.)"
He is never seen again and suspected victim of robbery and murder.)

Persons of Interest In Ann's Letters

Found in Letters

BARRICK, Eli, 15, 24
Soldier, 126 th Ohio Volun Infan,
Battle of Wilderness, Mar, 64
Body burned up after shot in head

BOWMAN, William, 1,2,3,13,21,23,26
Soldier, 126 th Ohio Volun Inf,
Prisoner, Andersonville, GA

DAVEY, Ruth J., 14
Friend, neighbor, letter writer/correspondent

HARPER, Maggie,
Friend of Daniel Huffman and Ann Letter A

HOOPINGARNER, Nick,
Friend of family, Brother of Wesley

HOOPINGARNER, Wesley, 15, 21, 26
Soldier, 126 th OVI,
neighbor,
Prisoner, turncoat

HILLICKS, George, 13
Soldier, Co L, 16 th Illinois Vol. Cavalry,
"FLAGSTAFF"
Subject of sketches of life in Andersonville Prison

HUFFMAN, Ann (Eve Anne) Many
    Sister of John J, David L, Daniel, George, Chrissey
    Responsible for the saving and collection of these letters

HUFFMAN, Christine J, (Chrissey),
    unmarried sister of Ann, 16, 21, 22, 24

HUFFMAN, Daniel,
    Brother to Ann,
    at home A, 4

HUFFMAN, David L.
    Soldier, 85 th Indiana Vol Inf 1, 2, 3, 6, 13, 25
    Brother of Ann, Chrissey, John J, George & Daniel,
    Multiple letters from war,
    Travelled with his brother, John,
    throughout the War.
    Killed in Goldsboro, NC, 3/25/65

HUFFMAN, David—also, an Uncle of Huffman boys, and Ann
    (letters from Bowman)

HUFFMAN, JOHN J, 4, 5, 10, 11, 12
    Soldier, 85 th Ind Vol Inf. 17, 19, 25, 27, 29
    Primary Soldier in this volume,
    Older brother of Ann, and David
    Many letters of guidance to Ann
    Paid Off June 28 th 1865 NEVER SEEN AGAIN
    He and David were in Sherman's Reserve Corp
    and the exclusive 20 th Corp during the Atlanta Campaign

HUFFMAN, Mathilda, (Till), 15,18, 23, 28
    Wife of brother George, at home with family

KIMMEL, Joseph W., 8, 9, 20, 29
    Soldier, 51 st Ohio Veteran Volunteer Inf.,
    Friend
    'Likes' Ann,

travels different path from the 126 th Regiment
Later, minister, starts churches
Letter

KIMMEL, Mary, 30
Friend of Ann,
family of Jos.W.

McCREERY, Catharine, 7
Friend of Ann,
cousin

PETERS, H.J.(Cpl)
Soldier, 126 th OVI,
Prisoner at Andersonville Prison
Later becomes Doctor,
Passed sketches of prison life along to other
126 th OVI members after Civil War
notes—sketches—Letter 13

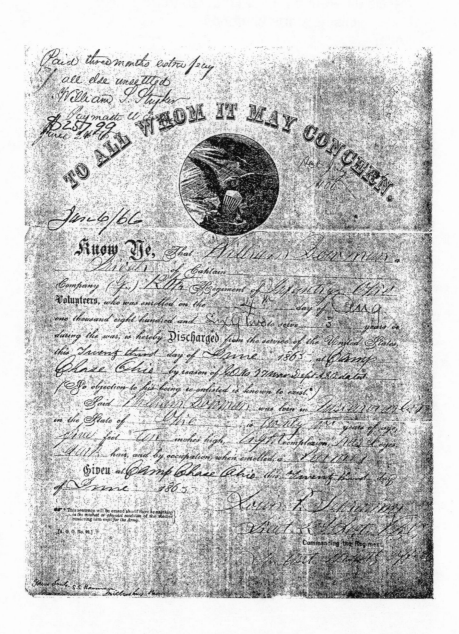

Discharge Papers, June 23, 1865, Wm Bowman

Oath of Identity, pension, Jan26'82, Wm Bowman